To Mike & Rindie —
May these pages
bring you
refreshment —

with love,
Joni
Grace

LifeSpace™

The practice of life with God

Joni Grace Powers & Robert Pyne

Regal

From Gospel Light
Ventura, California, U.S.A.

Published by Regal Books
From Gospel Light
Ventura, California, U.S.A.

Design by Celeste Rader-Philips.

Illustrations by Kevin Rechin.

Library of Congress Cataloging-in-Publication Data
Powers, Joni Grace.
    Lifespace : the practice of life with God / Joni Grace Powers and Robert Pyne.
        p. cm.
    Includes bibliographical references.
    ISBN 978-0-8307-4453-4 (hard cover) - ISBN 978-0-8307-4504-3 (international
trade paper)
    1. Spirituality. I. Pyne, Robert A. II. Title.
    BV4501.3.P695 2007
    248.4-dc22

2007007557

Dedication

I dedicate this book with love
to Tim, my cheerleader and unflagging supporter,
to Hannah, my West Texas soul mate,
to Kate, my eternal sunshine,
and to my parents, who led me to the Lord.
May this effort bring glory to God alone.

Joni Grace

For Julie, Steve, Danny, Ben and Becky,
and for my parents, Jim and Lois —
gifts of God whom I love dearly.

Bob

TABLE OF CONTENTS

chapter one

AZE

breathing

We write this book for all who need to breathe. We believe God intends for us to experience this life as an ever-expanding gulp of fresh air. So we write for the desperate: those heaving and gasping for breath. Maybe your breathing has become shallower each day, constricted after years of spiritual asthma. Or perhaps you have recently come to faith in God. You anticipated a promised surge of new life, but languish instead, bereft like a sailboat without wind.

• • • • • a story from Joni

I started breathing again in my mid-forties. My life with God the decades before resembled walking pneumonia: the breath slowly draining out of me until I clawed for air. A friend and I were hiking the Virginia hills when my lungs began to clear.

Patsy and I see each other only a few times each year. Within minutes of meeting, we whisk past chitchat and dive deep into weighty topics. Yes, we talk about existential questions such as why we exist. We also give equal time to vital issues like coloring or not coloring our hair.

At the top of one climb, God drenched us in a beautiful fall vista. Broad brushstrokes of color dazzled us. Patsy and I spread our arms wide and spun around in the mottled sunlight. We kicked leaves over each other and struck model-esque poses on God's grand stage. A boulder became a viewing stand.

Giddiness stilled as we drank in the view. Our quiet was partly awe. God's creation shimmered in its fall clothes. Yet a strange melancholy leached into the moment. Gazing outward, I wondered aloud: "Why does God seem so large up here? So glorious up here that I am almost blinded? So much about Life with a capital L up here? And why does hiking down this hill inevitably plunge me headlong into less life, small life, suffocating life? Life with a lower case 1. A pitiful excuse for life that feels a lot like death most days." *There we sat: two pilgrims expert in capitalizing on the promise of abundant life. Childhoods steeped in Christianity topped off with expensive seminary educations. Two people supposedly guiding other wanderers in their spiritual journeys. We wanted to lay our faces against the coolness of that boulder and never leave. Let the wind rustle through our hair. Revel in the space to breathe. After a while we peered down into shadows. Darkness eased onto the hills. We reluctantly adjourned to a cabin porch, but our wondering continued late into the night. Patsy and I sketched on napkins stolen from underneath glasses of big, bold red wine. Those napkins captured the seeds of thought that grew into this book.*

           ●   ●   ●   ●   ●

A church catechism asks, "What is the chief end of humanity?" It answers, "The chief end of humanity is to glorify God and enjoy God forever." The person of God populates the expanse in which we find our being. God intends to stake out the whole of our lives: every breath we take and every corner of our space, introducing unbounded joy in God's infinite loveliness.

A fully human life is an existence that reflects the knowledge of God and trust in God through an expansive experience of living. "Expansive" may sound dangerous. It suggests unending movement in many directions, surpassing a singular path from point A to point B. An interstate highway map will not help. This kind of life moves from a center ever outward versus from a boundary ever inward. Engaging the whole of God begs for spaciousness.

This life is ours for the taking:
an engorgement of air that
regenerates, revives and renews.
So why does life often feel anything but expansive?
Why are we suffocating?

We write for all who want to encounter anew—or perhaps for the first time—the life-giving breath of the Creator. We invite you to practice breathing with us as we enter into authentic relationship with the person of God. The ideas found here are not novel but ancient. We pray the Spirit of God will use the words on these pages to usher you into delight beyond measure.

glorifying

Expansive life centers on the eternal God. This statement represents the critical starting point for a fully human existence. God spoke through the prophet Isaiah, revealing the created purpose for humanity: "Bring my sons from far away and my daughters from the end of the earth—everyone who is called by my name, whom I created for my glory, whom I formed and made."

This mandate clearly claims God's preeminence as Creator. Called by God's name and created for God's glory, we bring honor and esteem to God as we reflect God's character. This purpose is not an egotistical move on God's part. God did not create us out of lack or vacuous need but out of a hospitable outpouring of the divine being.

Our next chapter, "Dirt," celebrates glory as the sum of God's perfections. Let us give you a foretaste of the splendor. Listen to scripture speak:

Bless the LORD, O my soul.
O LORD my God, you are very great.
You are clothed with honor and majesty,
wrapped in light as with a garment.

•   •   •   •   •

He determines the number of the stars;
he gives to all of them their names.
Great is our Lord, and abundant in power;
his understanding is beyond measure.

•   •   •   •   •

I blessed the Most High,
and praised and honored the one who lives forever.
For his sovereignty is an everlasting sovereignty,
and his kingdom endures from generation to generation.

•   •   •   •   •

In the beginning, Lord, you founded the earth,
and the heavens are the work of your hands;
they will perish, but you remain. . . .
You are the same, and your years will never end.

•   •   •   •   •

That God—eternal, powerful, creative, sovereign, majestic, unchanging—made us to reflect glory. That God, out of love, created us for relationship with the divine. That *love* calls us to expansive life.

Moses had a unique glimpse of God that helps us understand the relational nature of glory. The story unfolds in Exodus 33. The Israelites shunned God repeatedly, ignoring their redemption from slavery in Egypt and God's ongoing care for their lives. As a result, God refused to go with them into their new land, saying essentially, "If I went with you, I would have to kill you." The people balked at Moses' leadership, fought among themselves and were generally unruly. Moses desperately sought encouragement as he attempted to lead the exasperating people.

Wandering in the desert with the whining, rebellious Israelites used up all the resources Moses could muster. They sucked the air right out of him. Moses needed a reality larger than the circumstances he saw on the ground. He pleaded to see the fullness of God's glory in order to renew his belief in Life with a capital *L*.

You may know the story. God shielded Moses in the cleft of a rock and then passed by, proclaiming:

> The LORD, the LORD God, compassionate and gracious, slow to anger, and abounding in lovingkindness and truth; who keeps lovingkindness for thousands, who forgives iniquity, transgression and sin; yet He will by no means leave the guilty unpunished, visiting the iniquity of fathers on the children and on the grandchildren to the third and fourth generations.

This portrait revealed the personal God as the definition of love, forgiveness, justice and grace. Moses' reaction proved utterly appropriate. He "made haste to bow low toward the earth and worship."

After Moses came down from the mountain, his face shone with divine light. He literally glowed after a mere glimpse of God. The people shied away in fright, so Moses had to wear a veil over his head!

The God of Moses is the same God who pursues a relationship with us. A relational, personal God who reigns supreme over the universe. A God who defines what it is to be real.

To glorify God, we as human beings must embrace the divine reality greater than ourselves, reaching through and past the facts of our daily lives into an infinitely broader perspective. What does it look like to thrive in a life with God? As with Moses, the answer comes from beyond us.

Being made in the image of God to reflect the **Worth**
person of God defines your worth. There is no oth- beyond
er yardstick. The latest promotion or lack thereof, measure
a spouse or lack thereof, or the fact that your pastor
of ten years still cannot remember your name does not
define your worth. We sin as we chase reputation and value
rooted in our own glory. The Most Valuable One calls you into
relationship for eternity solely because the image of divine
glory shines through you. The world's measures hold no sway
with God.

You walk above circumstance, knowing that the **Identity**
facts evident to your eyes are not the whole beyond
picture. To be identified as a reflection of God circumstance
means circumstances cannot possess ultimate
power *over* you or *for* you. Your circumstances do not
define who you are. This cannot be a pull-yourself-up-by-
the-bootstraps gospel, urging you to wrench yourself out of the
gutter and make something of yourself. Nor can there be any
illusion that choice circumstances come your way because you
lassoed luck with sheer star-power. We sin when we succumb to
the siren call of circumstance as the end of all truth. God moves
in and among creation, working the divine plan of redemption.
You are graciously invited to participate.

Life with God brings love out of grace: unmerited, **Love**
undeserved favor. You cannot earn the love. God beyond
is the love. You are the blessed recipient called to performance
graciously pass it along. Too often the world doles
out love with strings attached. Your mother expects you
for dinner every Sunday as payback for putting you through college. Your boss likes you because you work sixty-hour weeks.

Your brother punished you with silence until you loaned him the money for a new car. We sin in loving as though life is a mathematical equation that has to balance. God does not own a calculator.

Only out of God's gracious love do we bask in a glorious relationship with the Holy One who dwells in unapproachable light and, like Moses, live to tell the tale. Jesus Christ, the Son of God, came to redeem us out of sin "to present you holy, without blemish, and blameless." Through Christ, there is peace between humanity and God. Our relationship is sealed for eternity. This life is about learning to live in the spaciousness of divine love. The romantic poet William Blake described this well:

> And we are put on earth a little space,
> That we may learn to bear the beams of love ...
> For when our souls have learn'd the heat to bear,
> The cloud will vanish; we shall hear his voice.

God, who is beyond measure, is the reason for our being. We act like prisms, refracting the beams of love to reflect glory back to our Creator. How do we retreat from that expansive picture of life to a small, constricted existence?

reducing

Our friend Sam will tell you life is good. He lives in Manhattan in a renovated Soho warehouse. His job has unlimited upside potential for creative work. Sam's group of friends volunteers on Saturdays to help maintain the historical district. A girlfriend hovers on the periphery of the picture, providing companionship without much maintenance required.

The parents come visit. They like to take the ferry around the Statue of Liberty. Sam buys the tickets, and they act surprised every time. Sam tips cabdrivers generously and steps around instead of on the homeless.

There is no need for God as far as Sam can tell. Things are fine. Sam left God behind in his hometown church when he packed for college. He might duck into a holiday service a few times a year, for old time's sake mostly. If not, no big deal. Holidays happen again next year. Things are fine. There is no need. Sam presents a sharp contrast from Moses desperately seeking God's face. Do we wish crisis or calamity on Sam so he sees a place for God? So God can be rescuer or welfare agent? No. There has to be Life with a capital *L* that applies to Sam just as it applies to the woman with breast cancer and three kids under the age of five whose husband died in the war. God must exist for both at the same time.

Unlike Sam, the Israelites in the Old Testament were certainly connected to God. They literally followed God out of Egypt and were hand-fed every meal in forty years of desert wandering. God was their only means of survival. But the people's hearts were fickle. One day they worshipped; the next they blasphemed.

The Old Testament prophets had thankless jobs. They usually arrived on the scene just in time to deliver a message of judgment, doom and destruction. Sometimes they were naked. It was not a job after which people clamored.

God used the prophets to call the people back from the brink of idolatry over and over. Sometimes people listened. Other times they thumbed their noses and ran the other way. Jeremiah, tough as nails, delivered an indictment from God:

Has a nation changed its gods, even though they are no gods? But my people have changed their glory for something that does not profit. Be appalled, O heavens, at this, be shocked, be utterly desolate, says the LORD, for my people have committed two evils: they have forsaken me, the fountain of living water, and dug out cisterns for themselves, cracked cisterns that can hold no water. Jeremiah 2

For some of us, like God's people of old, our elevated egos attempt to unseat God's glory. There are two steps here: forsaking God as the fountain of life and changing gods in the belief that we can create something better—career, family, home, money, reputation, church, health—the list goes on. We withdraw from the source of Life and Breath by making ourselves the epicenter of being. We chase pleasure only to be robbed of joy.

Eighteenth-century theologian Jonathan Edwards wrote of the "excellent enlargedness" of the human soul that resulted from the Creator's breath. Tragically, human sin—the love of that which is less than God—reversed the expansive direction of life.

> All this excellent enlargedness of man's soul was gone; and thenceforward he himself shrank, as it were, into a little space, circumscribed and closely shut up within itself to the exclusion of all things else....God was forsaken, and fellow creatures forsaken, and man retired within himself.

For all have sinned and fall short of the glory of God.

Romans 3

No one is exempt from the reductive effects of sin. We all chase lesser loves, even those of us who profess to be children of God. The suffocating clutch of death lurks in the wings, waiting for us to drop our gaze.

Our life with God can be stymied by indifference, as with Sam. Or perhaps we choose blatant rebellion, profaning the character of God. Often times, however, our sin is more subtle. Our gaze shifts from God's glorious grace to ourselves and our human effort. We accept the free gift of salvation, yet we strongly suspect that our own works earn God's ongoing love.

We measure spiritual maturity primarily by how well we avoid what we label as sin. The "narrow way" becomes a list of rules and behaviors for wearing a Christian nametag.

Shiny medals awarded for good conduct make us sparkle in our own brilliance. Instead of gulping breaths of life, we systematically box ourselves into the very opposite of abundance. Grace appears almost offensive in its freedom. The space for practicing life with God shrinks and contracts.

· · · · · **stop a moment**

Imagine that we are in the room with you now. Bob holds a large roll of masking tape. Joni stands next to you and begins to ask you some questions. "What political party do you support? Should Christians run for political office? What is your position on abortion? Should single mothers adopt children? Is poverty due to laziness? Is there just war? Can someone be a conscientious objector?" As you answer each question, Bob pulls off a strip of tape and puts it on the floor. The first four questions build a box with you standing inside. Bob then starts to place lines of tape that crisscross the box. You move inside each line.

Joni's questions shift a bit. "Do you go to church? How often? Should women be deacons? Does depression show a lack of faith? Does illness come from hidden sin? What about infertility? Do you believe the gift of tongues still exists? What about healing? Do you have an accountability partner? Are you tithing ten percent of your income? Before taxes? Is the Eucharist the real body of Christ or is it symbolic? Should the American flag be in your sanctuary?" Bob lays down more lines. The box becomes smaller and smaller. The space is getting crowded. You try to balance on your tiptoes.

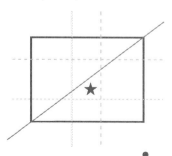

· · · · · ·

We construct our life with God by drawing lines of expected and acceptable opinions and behaviors. Fearing spiritual formation might be willy-nilly without sufficient control, we build a box to manage the process. With each sermon, each Bible study, each retreat, each small-group meeting, we add another line inside the box. Another position to be spiritual: Patriotism equals godliness. Another activity: Volunteer in Kids Clubs on Wednesday nights at church. Another rule: Journaling is mandatory. Another behavior: Achieve fifteen minutes of quiet time on your knees in your closet with the door closed before the sun rises.

Instead of loving God, we come to love our own construction of what we deem worthy of our attention. A list of rules replaces abundant life. We call out to passersby, "Here! Come be with me! Look at the fabulous life I have with God. Put on your toe shoes and tiptoe over here! Careful not to step on the lines. I put a lot of work into those."

Here is a crazy example of boxy thinking we heard recently. If you own a Subaru four-wheel drive car, then you must be an environmental activist. If you are an environmental activist, then you must be a Democrat. Since all Democrats are liberals who do not believe in God, obviously you are not a Christian. How about that box!

We asked teenagers in our church youth group how their peers at school know they are Christians. That was easy: no parties, no drugs, no alcohol, no sex, no cursing, no cheating, no R-rated movies. These young people have the box down pat. You could hear the masking tape ripping off the roll.

What a bizarre way to fabricate a life. Someone like Sam, watching us place lines on the floor, might wonder why we choose to live in these boxes of our own making. There are a myriad of reasons, really. We think we control the lines, and we crave control. We choose perceived safety over freedom. We impose capricious rules on one another, inevitably neglecting the law of love. Like the picture we drew, we each become a star in our own box.

Here is a hard truth. After the initial flurry of taping, we move into a maintenance mode. We become line monitors, going over and over the lines to keep them straight and neat, growling at people who dare step on them. We take shallow breaths to conserve oxygen in the small space. We push against others who try to put us in *their* boxes. Growth and delight disappear in the process. Life becomes stale. No wonder this box building drains life's breath out of us—it can be an exhausting, fulltime job!

We presume upon God's patience. This presumption treads in dangerous territory. Isaiah delivered a warning to the Israelites: "I am the LORD, that is My name; I will not give My glory to another." God is Lord over all and will not tolerate worship of lesser loves. We are to reflect God's image, not ours.

The heavens are telling of the glory of God;
and their expanse is declaring the work of His hands.

Psalm 19

• • • • • a story from Bob

For many years, I glanced over my shoulder continuously. I wanted to be sure God was watching me. I could have been the groundskeeper on a baseball field laying very precise, straight lines. Call me Mr. Discipline. Me inside the lines. Sin outside the lines. If I walked with the Spirit, I avoided sin and earned God's pleasure. If I sinned, God's face would turn away from me.

I participated in an organization in college that made the spiritual life feel like a competition. Each week we met to report such successes as our cumulative minutes of quiet time and the results of our evangelism efforts. Actual conversions to Christianity won extra points. Scripture memory was like a poetry slam. When I quoted a verse, the next person would quote a chapter. The crowning achievement was the woman who quoted Psalm 119. We were all in awe!

When I started teaching at seminary, I focused on laying down yet another set of lines. Truth inside. Untruth outside. Defending the faith became the primary thrust. On that battlefield, grace found scarce room to breathe. I was convinced that my box remained quite a bit larger than many of my colleagues'. I told students, "The world is not black and white. There are shades of gray." I felt sophisticated saying that.

As I look back over the years, I feel slivers of sadness. The slivers come from opportunities lost. I had extensive knowledge of theology and expended enormous effort maintaining my box. At times scant energy remained for the most important tasks: loving God and loving others well. I encouraged my students as nimble scholars, but I did not appreciate God's concern for the affections of their hearts. I was far too easily satisfied with smallness. God is now graciously showing me that shades of gray pale in comparison to life in technicolor.

•   •   •   •   •

Whether it is Sam with a fine life that has no place for God, or the rebellious people who know God but are harlots with their love, or the earnest builders of boxes, all are staring at their own navels in self-love. Humanity's purpose for being, ordained by God, reduces to a shadow as the gaze takes a hard turn inward.

There is so much more, and we have no idea what we are missing.

But hope reigns.

expanding

They feast on the abundance of your house,
and you give them drink from the river of your delights.
For with you is the fountain of life;
in your light we see light.

Psalm 36

As our lives reclaim the excellent enlargedness of our created purpose, God intends delight. In the process of writing this book, we took a group of editors out to the Powers' family place in west Texas. Some of us knew each other prior to the trip. Others were strangers. We spent several days sharpening the manuscript between bookends of breathtaking sunrises and sunsets.

The last morning we scrambled up a pink granite mountain behind the ranch house. A panoramic view rewarded our effort. The wind snapped at our coats and gave us crazy hairdos. Bob was looking for a herd of wild mountain sheep known to bed down on the summit. We saw signs of them, but our sheep calls went unanswered.

We found a flat rock overlooking the southern exposure. Joni opened her backpack and laid out the elements of communion. A cloth from Kenya with golden threads set the table. Rocks anchored the corners. An antique china plate and cup from a great aunt held the bread and wine. We read the Word of God as the pages of the Bible fluttered in the wind.

"This is my body . . . my blood . . . do this . . . in remembrance of me."

Each person—Sandi, Reg, Laurie, Sara, Miriam and both of us—looked around the circle. Sisters and brothers in Christ with knees touching on top of a blustery peak. Strangers no more. Tied together through the blood of Christ for eternity.

Experiencing God's reality beyond the mountain, the rock, the sky, the cloth, the china, the bread, the wine. Beyond us. The air curled and twirled and the Holy Spirit moved. Embodied, expansive life happened.

God had a final missive of delight. The herd of sheep waited until we were off the mountain and then bounded up the side of the hill in full view of our cameras. We laughed at their leaping and jumping over the very boulders we had just climbed. God graciously brought us joy.

Through the reconciling work of Christ, God provides the means for great intakes of life's breath. There is space to truly live expansively. Expanding joy. Expanding love. Expanding knowledge. Expanding faith. We draw outward from the center as we delight in the whole of God. The image is not one of tape on the floor but one of an ever-expanding sphere.

Have you seen a toy called the Hoberman Sphere®? It starts out as a closed ball. As you pull its sides, the sphere expands in all directions with space inside and out. The manufacturer makes these large enough to accommodate a person inside. The big spheres have a mind of their own. Watch out when one starts to unfold on you!

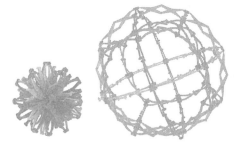

The closed sphere represents the incurvature of self-love. We live with hard edges, withholding forgiveness and hoarding our time and resources for selfish gain. As the Holy Spirit transforms our affection for God, the sphere begins to expand. We open up to allow God's character of love to shine through us like light shining through the openings of the sphere. The edges begin to soften.

Just as the sphere enlarges and expands, our life starts to reflect a joy bounded only by our boundless God, transcending circumstances. We live Life with a capital *L* in a reality beyond ourselves. The enlarging sphere invites a radical and liberating change in our gaze. A gaze curved inward in self-love shifts to look up and out to the loveliness of the person of God and onward through God toward our fellow human beings.

When we use a large sphere as a visual aid in teaching, typically the participants' eyes widen as it opens outward. They unconsciously take a deep breath that follows the expansion. When we collapse the sphere, you see distress and disappointment on their faces. Breathing was such a treat while it lasted!

One pastor had an almost allergic reaction. "Without a box, how do I control my people?" Living out of God's gracious love can be a scary place. It requires faith in God's purposes and methods and the humility to admit addiction to the perceived safety of masking tape. The terrifying embrace of grace grips you as air rushes into your lungs.

> Sin is the suicidal abandonment of joy.
>
> John Piper

Choosing self-love, in whatever form it takes, ignores the very source of our delight. It is a choice for death over life. That is why John Piper, a pastor and theologian passionate about the delight of God's glory, calls sin "the suicidal abandonment of joy." When the gaze shifts away from us and our efforts to the person of God, obedience becomes rightly seated in the commandments to love God and to love others with reckless abandon.

Our lives move toward an excellent enlargedness once again through the transforming power of the Spirit of God. (Our fifth chapter, "Shift," describes this process.) We begin to turn away from self-centeredness. We put away the masking tape. We quell our rebellion. We engage in a relationship with the divine that spills out onto the people around us. The Spirit enables us to delight first and foremost in the One truly worthy of our adoration: God. From that expansive center, we move to what God loves and how God loves.

Remarkably, this process will never end. As finite creatures of an infinite God, we will never know the depth of God's mysteries. Our delight cannot exhaust the breadth of loveliness. Throughout eternity, we will enjoy new illuminations of God. The sphere will ever expand!

· · · · · **stop a moment**

The sphere is a metaphor that we will use throughout the book. You need one of your own. Get one wherever cool toys are sold. Play with the sphere. Watch it expand. Think about life with God as expanding like the sphere. Do you use lines to draw a box around your life with God? What are they? Are you indifferent to God? How did you come to that place? Practice breathing deeply each time you pull the sphere open. How does it feel to watch the sphere close? Imagine life as an expanding sphere that has no end!   · · · · ·

In this chapter, we introduce the idea of expansive life. We begin to reclaim the space to practice life with God. Hopefully you have found yourself in these pages already.

The following chapters begin with the glory of God at the center of the sphere and expand the topics from there. We visit such issues as why being fully human is our greatest calling, how the incarnation of Jesus Christ matters in the present, and what is a realistic view of the Holy Spirit.

Next we explore the oft-misunderstood and much-ignored law of love. We talk about the complexion of our joy in God; the community of humans as God's agents for change; God's love demonstrated in grace, forgiveness and sacrifice; and our peculiar standing as a people of hope.

Remember to breathe as you work through the concepts. New perspectives will come fast and hard. Stay with it. The topics build upon each other and circle into each other. We constantly loop back to show you how it all fits together.

You will not find five easy steps to spiritual maturity or six disciplines leading to nirvana. We want to think well together in order that we may love well together. Neither objective is simple. Putting this material into a flat dimension such as a book is both a great privilege and an ongoing frustration. We wish we could sit beside you and hear your stories in a live, embodied conversation. We hope someday we will have the blessing of doing just that. Until then, we pray over your reading.

Use the white space in this book to jot notes, pose questions or doodle as you ponder the ideas we present. The space gives you breathing room. You will not be penalized for marking in the book. It will not self-destruct.

May the Holy Spirit illuminate your path. May our words bring only good to you. May our humble effort be used by the Spirit to lead you to deeply satisfying gulps of fresh air.

I pray that the God of our Lord Jesus Christ,

the Father of glory,

may give you a spirit of wisdom and revelation

as you come to know him,

so that, with the eyes of your heart enlightened,

you may know what is the hope

to which he has called you,

what are the riches of his glorious inheritance

among the saints,

and what is the immeasurable greatness

of his power for us who believe,

according to the working of his great power.

Ephesians 1

LifeSpace

chapter two

IRT

the question

Our families recently traveled to Africa for ministry among the people of Rwanda. We spent a few days in sturdy canary-yellow trucks as we drove on safari among the wild animals. Picture an enormous zoo without fences and not a cage in sight. The drivers had one rule: "Stay in the vehicle." Duly noted.

At one point, we lingered to watch a cheetah feed on a fresh kill. We could hear his teeth split bones and shred muscle. He licked his lips as blood dripped on the dirt. We winced with each crunch. Someone in the truck whispered, "Makes you want to be a vegetarian, doesn't it?" Sharing meat-eater status with the cheetah seemed less than appetizing at that moment. A bit too earthy for our taste. The humans felt tangible relief sitting inside the vehicles while the animals were out.

Often a discussion of humanity begins with a survey of what humans are in contrast to what other creatures are not. Give people a few minutes and a list inevitably emerges. We walk upright. We reason. We demonstrate emotion. We paint our toenails. Eating meat would not set us apart from the cheetah, so that cannot go on the list. If you have enough people in the discussion, someone will disagree with every item. Whales talk to each other. Chimps solve problems. Elephants keen over their dead. Poodles paint their toenails. Humans are not unique.

We suggest that any discussion of humanity beginning with "What am I?"—over and against what other creatures are not—starts in the wrong place. In the previous chapter, we quoted a church catechism: "What is the chief end of humanity? The chief end of humanity is to glorify God and enjoy God forever." This starting point shifts the question from "What am I?" to "Why am I?" By seeking God's purpose in our creation, we then discover the essence of being human.

We introduced an unknown object to a classroom of students recently. "What is it?" we asked.

The object in question looked like an open triangle about five inches wide. If made of metal, it could have been an old-fashioned dinner bell. The dense, white foam triangle had an opening at the top. The object would open and close like a clamp if you pinched it from the bottom.

Why am I?

"Must be some kind of clip. Maybe it fastens a tablecloth to a picnic table."

"But why foam? I'm thinking it's a chunk of packing material."

"Seems too fancy for that. It looks like a piece of the space shuttle."

The guesses became more far-fetched with each passing minute. The students reached for the object's packing box.

"A Door Mouse."

Knowing its name still did not help. A picture on the box solved the mystery. The foam triangle was made to fit over the edge of a door, preventing it from closing on a toddler's fingers. Once they knew its purpose, the students could identify the object as a child safety device. What a far cry from a chunk of the space shuttle!

Purpose or function also identifies the creature we call human. We share many similarities with other creatures. Physical appearance or genetic makeup does not sufficiently differentiate humans; rather our purpose to enjoy God and delight in God for eternity marks us as unique. That purpose defines what it is to be human.

> To be human is the highest calling
> in the created world.
> Becoming fully human
> is our greatest hope.

Grab a pen. If someone asked you to do a spontaneous word association with the term "human," what would you say? What words immediately come to mind? Jot down the words in the space provided below. Stay with it until you have at least ten words. Go ahead. The next sentence will wait.

_____   _____

_____   _____

_____   _____

_____   _____

_____   _____

Now look at your list (the blanks you just filled in, right?). What does it say about your view of being human? If someone looked at your list, what image would they see?

Here is another perspective on this exercise. Consider that God became human as Jesus Christ the Son. Circle any words that you would apply to the incarnated God. Are any words not circled?

• • • • •

the image

The Lord God formed the first human from the dust of the ground and breathed into virgin nostrils the breath of life. Take a little dirt, infuse a God-sized breath and out comes humanity. Our children tell us we are old as dirt. The local gossip wants to give us the dirt. Your grandmother yells if you track in the dirt.

Can the highest calling in the created world come from such an earthy beginning?

The answer to that question does not depend on the quality of the soil. In Genesis 1, "God created humankind in his image, in the image of God he created them; male and female he created them." David pondered that creative act when he spoke of humanity being "crowned with glory and honor" in Psalm 8. He did not suggest that we should stare at our own navels in awe. The psalm begins and ends with the gaze on God. "O LORD, our Lord, how majestic is your name in all the earth!" David asked of God, "What are human beings that you are mindful of them?" His tone reveals wonder. God the Creator bestowed glory and honor, so any perspective on humanity must, like the psalm, begin and end with God. The primary question becomes, "What is God?"

The biblical language describing God deals in perfections. The sum of these personal perfections or attributes makes up the broad concept of God's glory.

God is . . .

Transcendent . . . distinct from and sovereign over all creation.

Immanent . . . intimately involved in all creation.

Eternal . . . exists as the essence of life.

Infinite . . . all-knowing, ever-present, all-powerful.

Free . . . independent in will and activity.

Unchanging . . . forever permanent.

Holy . . . completely other and separate in perfections.

True . . . consistent in being and activity.

Righteous . . . perfect in relationship to all.

Jealous . . . protective of exclusive divinity.

Loving . . . gracious, merciful, just, faithful, good, compassionate.

What moved this glorious God, the definition of all that is real and perfect, to create anything? Complete in all respects, God was neither lonely nor lacking. Theologian Robert Jenson, who writes insightfully on human purpose, described creation as an act of hospitality. "God as Father, Son, and Spirit can make room in himself for others, and the room that he makes is our created time. The opening of that room is the act of creation."

Paul wrote of God, "For *from* Him and *through* Him and *to* Him are all things. To Him be the glory forever." God created all things for God's own pleasure and for the sake of the only being in existence—God. In the words of theologian John Calvin, the universe is "a theatre of God's glory" created out of the overflowing effluence of the divine being.

Such language makes many people uncomfortable. We label a person who pursues fame above all else "egotistical" or "arrogant." Mirror, Mirror, on the wall, who is the fairest of them all? However, being the definition of perfection, God alone *deserves* utmost regard. It would be profane for God to value anything more.

Reflecting the divine image, we are called to worship and enjoy the whole of God. We will never be transcendent, but we can appreciate and rest in God's sovereignty over the whole of creation. We are not the eternal source of life, but we live by the grace of God's breath.

We can and do manifest other aspects of glory. We reflect the love of God as agents of grace, purveyors of mercy, initiators of forgiveness, champions of justice, demonstrators of faithfulness, lovers of the good and fountains of compassion. We bring a breath of fresh air as life-givers, reserving the space for our fellow human beings to breathe and grow. The chapters titled "Rope," "Space," "Gift" and "Fool" talk more about what this looks like.

God invites us into a relationship distinct from the rest of creation. German theologian Karl Barth, in his extensive study of humanity, observed: "The creature's right and meaning and goal and purpose and dignity lie—only—in the fact that God as the Creator has turned toward it with His purpose." We participate together with God in the enjoyment of divine glory.

the point

Why does this discussion of purpose and image matter to the next breath you take? It is lovely and inspiring, but we seem to spend our days trying to overcome the very thing we were created to be: human.

Understanding *why* we exist must inform *how* we exist.

We live to fulfill our created purpose
rather than transcend it.

Our beginning as dirt animated by the divine breath intertwines our existence between earth and heaven. It is an odd and confusing place to stand at times.

• • • • • a story from Joni

Being human had always seemed like a temporary gig in my book. I would romp through the corridors of this life, hopefully die without whining and then head on up to heaven. The main point on this earth was to avoid embarrassing God or my family. Heaven would entail hanging out near God's throne, wearing my sunglasses in the brilliant light.

I embraced the idea of being a "godlet" in heaven. I would get all the "omnis" that God enjoys: omniscient and know everything, omnipresent and be everywhere, omnipotent and have all power. There was no way I would lug that humanity ball and chain around in heaven. Being human was a sin. Sin could not get past the Pearly Gates, so something had to change. I knew I would not be an angel. The whole halo-and-wing idea never did anything for me anyway. Kind of spooky and a little boring. I knew God would still be in charge. Godlet was the only job left.

A new dawn appeared as the Spirit of God faithfully brought me around to truth. I am human now and I will be human later. While this physical body will change in a fashion that I cannot describe, I will be in heaven, fully human, standing before God's throne. I have a list of wishes for the new body, but there is no telling whether I will be able to submit it.

There is no job opening for godlet. I cannot work my way into the job by winning an award for holiness. I am holy and I will ever be holy only by my connection to the holy God through Christ, the Son.

I will not change into another being or person finally freed from being Joni. Jenson said it well: "I am identical with myself across time, both now and in the Kingdom, not by virtue of what is within me but by virtue of what I am within, by virtue of specific location in the unbroken life of the Father, Son, and Spirit." This Joni will mirror God's glory, shining brightly without taint or shadow. My delight in the perfections of God starts now and will only increase for eternity, never stagnating.

This awakening liberates me and gives me space to practice this life with God. It brings me peace. The sphere expands. I plan to eat more ice cream in celebration.

● ● ● ● ●

One of our favorite authors, Barbara Brown Taylor, recently gave an interview about her years as a pastor. The interviewer recounted Taylor's statement that the call to serve God was first and foremost a call to be fully human. In response to the interviewer's query, Taylor clarified what she meant:

At the very least it would mean something about every day, to the best of my ability, resisting being a fake. Resisting the fake answer, the false front, the superficial conversation in favor of something more deeply human, more deeply connected to what really matters about being alive, whether it sounds religious or spiritual or correct or not. It means worrying less about being perfect and being concerned more with being authentic or real with other people. Much of the religion I was schooled in was about putting myself away, aside, behind me in order to become something holier and closer to God. In other words, to draw nearer to the Really Real I needed to be less me. Perhaps it was a mid-life revelation or just wearing out that led me to a different understanding that my humanity was God's chief gift to me and that if I was going to find the Really Real it was going to be within that and not separating myself from that. It meant that the holiest thing I could be was the flawed human being God had made me to be.

Perhaps being *fully human* sounds a bit nebulous and bordering on hedonistic. People will take a mile if given an inch. Who will be hall monitor? Indicting humanness as sin is one method we use to keep a lid on things down here. We will never fulfill our created purpose until we let go of that fallacy. To be fully human takes an immoderate, crazy love for all that is God and turns it upon all that is human.

Being human is not a problem to be overcome.

We are created in the divine image to participate like no other creature can in God's enjoyment of God. This truth yields radical implications. Every human being we see bears the weight of God's glory. Every person bears the mark of God's value and the dignity afforded in God's love for humanity. There are no dispensable or wasted human beings. In the words of author

C. S. Lewis, "your neighbor is the holiest object presented to your senses."

We blaspheme God's creative intent when we demean people of a different color, with a disability, with money or without, with education or without, in another church, not in any church, who are total strangers, or the cousin we shun because she is a lesbian—the list could go on.

A cashier at the local grocery store thanked Joni for turning off her cell phone and greeting him. His comment? "It sucks to be a cashier at a grocery store. It really sucks to be an *invisible* cashier." Pardon the language—just reporting the truth. A human being stands in front of us and yet we do not see him. Our vaunted technology can distance us from humans as often as it brings us closer.

Human beings can be inefficient and inelegant and gangly and awkward. We lurch around like newborn giraffes. We crash into others. We fall down. We cannot take care of ourselves. At the same time, human beings sing and dance and play and laugh and cry and share chocolate. We love well and love poorly.

Each one of us reflects our Creator: Some days the mirror is clear—other days, foggy. We gaze on God as our greatest love in one moment; we turn and run toward everything profane and unworthy in the next. But we are always, on all days, God's. Every single one of us. No one more and no one less than another.

We are embodied beings created in space and time.

The fully human life is a gift from God that involves your whole being and excludes no part of you. You might say, "Well, my spirit is all about God. My body, however, delivers Trouble with a capital *T*. Remember Jesus speaking about the spirit being willing but the flesh being weak? Sin would be a thing of the past if this traitorous bag of bones would quit following me around!"

Jesus said that rebellion against the affections of God comes from within each person—not from the body or from external objects. The body is not pure or even neutral since many of our selfish desires directly relate to bodily pleasures. However, neither is there a separate pure soul or spirit. Whatever we do, for good or for bad, we do as whole persons.

Life with God can be misunderstood to consist largely of bodily discipline. Paul urged young Timothy to resist such legalistic ideas. "They forbid marriage and demand abstinence from foods, which God created to be received with thanksgiving by those who believe and know the truth. For everything created by God is good, and nothing is to be rejected, provided it is received with thanksgiving; for it is sanctified by God's word and by prayer."

Spiritual discipline may rightly incorporate physical elements such as prayer postures, fasting or solitude to sharpen the gaze on God, but it must encompass more than those elements. Disciplines of loving ungainly humans well—such as grace, mercy and sacrifice—are also integral to being fully human.

Our friend Lilian Calles Barger noted, "If spiritual transcendence requires a flight from our body, then our spiritual journey is unstable, if not altogether impossible, because our body keeps crashing in on us." Further, "Since the body is the location in which spirituality is lived out, the richness of our spiritual life depends on how we view life cycles, aging, beauty, intimacy, illness, and finally our own death."

· · · · · stop a moment

Lauren Winner, a fresh voice on life with God, wrote an article on the most counter-cultural act for a Christian in this age. Her conclusion? Sleep. Yes, sleep. Such an act flies against our quest for twenty-four-hour days seven days a week. We admit to physical limitation. Sleep means we stand down from our tasks. Phone off. Computer dark. We acknowledge the need to rejuvenate and quit grasping for more as the sleepy minutes drift by in our dreams.

Do you deny the limitations of embodied life? How? Where do you pretend that you can transcend your humanity in this physical world? Is your schedule insane? Do you sleep? Enough? Do you have time to think or feel or listen? Does silence or stillness make you nervous? What can you do this week to celebrate your embodied existence?

• • • • •

We are under obvious constraints of space and time. We must submit to the sovereignty of God, who controls the means, the process and the timing of our lives. In return, the Holy Spirit moves us to delight in God's perfect provision. One moment that provision may be a sound, restful nap. The next moment may be a chase after a two-year-old grandson and his new puppy. All comes from God, through God and for God. The sphere expands.

• • • • • a story from Bob

For me, image was about the box. To reflect God meant conformity to a moral code of behavior. The better I maintained the box, the more glory God received. The idea of enjoying God seemed inconsequential—something at the end of things, after I wrapped up this life with a bow and marked it for delivery to heaven.

The Holy Spirit used Jonathan Edwards' book The End for Which God Created the World *to expand my view. I came to see that we are like God in that we are created to enjoy God. The Holy Spirit transforms our affections to love the beauty of God. I love Edwards' words:*

> *In the creature's knowing, esteeming, loving, rejoicing in, and praising God, the glory of God is both exhibited and acknowledged; his fullness is received and returned . . .*

The beams of glory come from God, are something of God, and are refunded back again to their original.

God's glorious attributes shine most brightly when they are both seen and celebrated. We participate, as no other creature apparently can, in God's enjoyment of God. The party will go on without me, but God has sent me a personal invitation.

So how do I practice being fully human by enjoying God? We mention a trip to west Texas in the first chapter. We happened upon a spectacular sunset on our way to the house. Thank goodness for the deserted road, because Joni immediately hit the brakes, and we all piled out to take in the scene. Reg threw himself down in the middle of the pavement and started shooting pictures. We posed with creation's fiery glory in the background.

We exclaimed over the hues of red, orange, yellow and pink as if we were watching fireworks bursting on the horizon. Oh! Ah! Wow! We breathed in the big sky. Lots of hugging and laughter ensued as we shared the sheer physicality of the experience. The moment hung pregnant with joy.

God threw a party for Life with a capital L. We exuberantly accepted the invitation!

One of my students heard me talking about the sunset after I returned from the trip. He commented, "The eternal sunshine of the delighted mind. Must be nice." I understood his skepticism. Delight can be illusive. Today in fact, as I write, a funk looms over my head. Long days of work and unresolved tensions with people in my life drive me to the isolated safety of my study. Curling into a fetal position under a blanket seems like an excellent option.

But God's invitation to joy remains just as real today as it was on that country road. I can turn inward into the abyss or I can look for options that pull my gaze outward. Maybe my daughter, Becky, wants to play catch with the football.

I am headed out to find the girl with the infectious giggle.

●　　●　　●　　●　　●

The Pynes' eldest son blesses us with a walking, talking lesson in how to be fully human. Steve has Down syndrome. There is no guile in any molecule of his being. What you see is what you get, with refreshing honesty. When asked to write a short autobiography at school, he began with the important information: "My name is Steve Pyne and I love God." What a gift of clarity. He demonstrates the *imago dei*, the image of God, in sharp relief. The Really Real of being human, deeply connected to what matters about being alive.

We desire to reflect the loveliness of God as creatures who both are and are becoming fully human. We embrace the messiness of this life as we practice what it is to live as fallible creatures in relationship with a holy God. We acknowledge the weight of glory that rests upon each and every person. We see being human as a calling, not a problem to be solved.

These confessions allow us to forsake the inward curvature of smallness for an outward expansion into our created purpose. Life with a capital *L* becomes possible here in the dirt. Amazingly, God loved us enough to come join us. God the Son came as both human and divine to be a bridge from earth to heaven. This mystery is the topic of the next chapter.

Since the display of God's glory
in our finite, creaturely experience
of knowing and delighting in God
is the aim of creation,
the achievement of this aim
will take all eternity—
there will never be a time
when there is no more glory
for the redeemed
to discover and enjoy.

John Piper

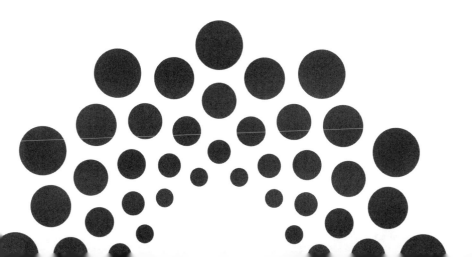

LifeSpace

chapter three

AY

For God so loved the world,
that he gave his only begotten Son,
that whosoever believeth in him
should not perish, but have everlasting life.

• • • • • a story from Joni

I grew up seriously Southern Baptist in far west Texas. We know how to do church out there: six hours on Sunday, Wednesday night Girls in Action (do not ask), weekend rallies at the high school stadium. It required Herculean stamina. John 3:16 was the first verse I memorized as a child. Evangelists might use a bead bracelet or a glove with fuzzy balls on the fingers or a wordless book to present the gospel of the Son to kids today. None of those props hold a candle to the Baptist craft wizards turned loose on John 3:16.

I still have a plaster cast of the earth painted in blue tempera paint, with stick people etched on it. A ragged, gold felt cross overlays the figures. My cross hangs off the earth because scissors challenged me at the time. Glue sticks had not yet been invented, so add massive globs of dried glue to the whole scenario. I remember eating the ubiquitous sugar cookies with the holes in the middle and drinking red punch to celebrate finishing the project. The teachers bribed us.

We kids recited John 3:16 by rote in a sing-song monotone. No big deal really: just God coming to earth in flesh and blood and saving us to eternal life. We sang, "Amazing grace, how sweet the sound, that saved a wretch like me. I once was lost, but now am found, was blind but now I see." The "wretch" part confused me. I assumed my brother must fit the description. I would rock back and forth in the pew, flipping the hymnal up and down with boredom.

I worry that I still approach the incarnated God with general malaise and a poverty of wonder. I struggle with what it means to follow the living Christ. God waits at the gate in heaven for me. The Son holds a colored flag like a tour director to make sure I queue up correctly. In the meantime, I slog through the muck on my own down here, delivering all the right words in rote monotone.

Here is the truth from me to you as I write this story: John 3:16 must be real for my very next breath or it cannot be real at all. Do not tell me that I have been snatched from the fiery tentacles of hell as if that is enough. That helps, but it is not enough. The plaster earth and stick people and felt cross will not suffice. The Son is alive and I want what he has. I want Life.

I shall make a simple move in the right direction. Today I will practice reciting John 3:16 as if it matters.

● ● ● ● ●

reconcile

The apostle Paul made a classic understatement when contemplating the incarnation of God: "Without any doubt, the mystery of our religion is great." Was Paul frowning or smiling as he wrote those words? Perhaps both at the same time? The book of Revelation pictures God sitting on a throne surrounded by flashes of lightning, with emerald rainbows blinding angelic hosts as they cry, "Holy, Holy, Holy is the Lord God Almighty!" Yet the gospel proclaims that this God showed up and joined us in the dirt.

God did not simply stop in for a visit like your rich aunt from New York City who bought you the toy your parents would never consider, only to swoop off on an airplane, leaving you spoiled rotten. God came down in the person of the Son and took on our humanity. The Son became fully human, while remaining fully God, forever. Why would he do such a thing?

In the beginning was the Word, and the Word was with God, and the Word was God. The Word became flesh and made his dwelling among us. We have seen his glory, the glory of the one and only [Son], who came from the Father, full of grace and truth. John 1

The Son, the preeminent Human Being, demonstrated the essence of what it is to be human. Christ perfectly reflected God's glory, fulfilling God's creative purpose for humanity. When we say that humanity is neither a problem to be solved nor something to be transcended, the incarnated God is the object lesson. In German theologian Dietrich Bonhoeffer's words:

> There is no more pretense, hypocrisy, cramped coercion to be something other than what one is, something better, something more ideal. God loves real human beings. God became a real human being.

Over and over in the Bible, we see God pursue humanity for relationship. That demonstration of faithful love points to the perfection of God's glory. Paul wrote in Ephesians 2:

> But God, who is rich in mercy, out of the great love with which he loved us even when we were dead through our trespasses, made us alive together with Christ.

Solely out of extravagant love for humanity, the person of the Son came to redeem us for God's own purposes. Solely out of lavish grace, Jesus Christ became the way back to God from the far places we wander. Solely out of bountiful mercy, God offers life abundant that breaks the bonds of our suffocating self-absorption.

· • • • • stop a moment

In the early centuries of the church, Christ's followers articulated their most basic beliefs through creeds or formal statements. The **Nicene Creed** captures orthodox belief about the triune person of God. We include the entirety of the creed on these pages as condensing it diminishes the richness.

We believe in one God,
the Father, the Almighty,
maker of heaven and earth,
of all that is, seen and unseen.
We believe in one Lord, Jesus Christ,
the only Son of God,
eternally begotten of the Father,
God from God, light from light,
true God from true God,
begotten, not made,
of one Being with the Father;
through him all things were made.
For us and for our salvation
he came down from heaven,
was incarnate of the Holy Spirit and the Virgin Mary
and became truly human.
For our sake he was crucified under Pontius Pilate;
he suffered death and was buried.
On the third day he rose again
in accordance with the Scriptures;
he ascended into heaven
and is seated at the right hand of the Father.
He will come again in glory to judge the living and the dead,
and his kingdom will have no end.
We believe in the Holy Spirit, the Lord, the giver of life,
who proceeds from the Father and the Son,
who with the Father and the Son is worshiped and glorified,
who has spoken through the prophets.
We believe in one holy catholic and apostolic Church.
We acknowledge one baptism for the forgiveness of sins.
We look for the resurrection of the dead,
and the life of the world to come. Amen.

Read the creed aloud several times. If you are sitting next to someone on an airplane, either read it silently or very loudly—who knows where the Holy Spirit may take you? Pay attention to each line. Let the words steep for a moment. Hesitate at every punctuation mark. You might even decide to memorize it for meditation. As followers of Jesus Christ joining with ancient voices, we invite you into this confession.

• • • • •

One God, maker of all that is seen and unseen, sent the Son for us and for our salvation. In the Son, through the Holy Spirit, we look for the resurrection of the dead and the life of the world to come. God saves us from indifference, from rebellion and from our own futile efforts to save ourselves.

The Word became flesh, Emmanuel, "God with us." Why that approach? God could have written, "HEY, I LOVE YOU! FROM, GOD" across the sky in gigantic twinkling stars—direct and to the point without all the mystery. That would have been impressive and might have held human attention for a millisecond or two. Instead of being content to reflect God's glory, we seek our own. We would soon scoff at the heavenly display. "Yeah, yeah. God is just showing off again. Always wanting the limelight. Look over here. I made this origami star out of cut-up leaves. Get a load of this! Pretty special, huh?"

We exchange the expansive glory of God to gaze at our own creations. This incurvature leads to a constricted existence, making our worth and identity dependent on the smallest perception of reality. We persist on a course into the abyss: forsaking the source of Life, careening down a path that leads away from being human. Our breath shrinks until we suck air through a tiny straw. We reject the fountain of Living Water for broken cisterns.

This is the essence of sin that alienates us from God. None of our offerings can erase our profanity against the sacred and satisfy the wrath of the Holy One. Old Testament priests slapped lamb after lamb and bull after bull on the altar. Steaming blood cascaded over the cold stone. It could never be enough.

The unique presence of humanity and divinity in Jesus Christ establishes him as the perfect mediator for restoring the relationship between God and humans. Christ satisfied the wrath of God for eternity through the spilling of life-blood on a cross. God returned the Son to life through resurrection from the tomb. Jesus declared, "I am the resurrection and the life. Those who believe in me, even though they die, will live." He is the way, the portal to Life with a capital *L*.

We persist on a course into the abyss

Through Christ, we are saved from alienation and brought to righteousness—being rightly related to the Creator God. Peace reigns once again. We are no longer strangers and aliens, but fellow citizens with the saints, children in God's household.

• • • • • stop a moment

First, take a minute to breathe through your nose, as our nurse friend recommends when someone is hyperventilating. The last few pages should feel weighty. You might want to reread them before moving ahead.

Now envision yourself standing before the throne of God. Give yourself time to survey the entire scene. There are no pictures available, so you will have to use your imagination. Do you see darkness or light or both? If there is light, what is its source? Are there physical bodies in the room? Are you in a physical body? Is anyone else with you or are you alone with God? What is your posture? What is God's posture toward you? Are you close to the throne or far away? Does God's face have an expression? Does yours? Is anyone speaking? If so, what is the tone of voice? What is being said? What do you think will happen next?

Use the space below to jot notes about what you see and hear in this imagining.

_____

_____

_____

_____

What do your answers say about how you see Christ? Is he present in your picture? Where is Christ in relationship to you? What does it look like to be redeemed in Christ as you stand before the throne of God?

• • • • •

imagine

You will stand in the throne room of God only because the incarnated God stood in the dirt with humans. We meet Christ at the intersection of dirt and sky, now and later.

The Son of God did not bring a piece of God to earth; he *was* God on earth. Likewise the Son of God did not come as the shadow or pretense of a human; he was *fully* human. Jesus did not simply put on the clothes of humanity, draping embodied life over his shoulders like a cloak.

If we see the Son primarily as the highest moral example and master teacher, we risk missing the point of God's embodiment. We strip away the uncomfortable dimensions of the Son's humanity: laughing and crying; being hungry and dirty; yearning for different circumstances; refereeing the antics of the disciples who would launch into bickering over who sat where at the table. Bonhoeffer continued writing about the Really Real: "Jesus Christ is not the transfiguration of high humanity, but God's yes to real human beings."

Remember the word list you generated in the previous chapter on the term "human"? We asked you to circle the words you would apply to Jesus. Turn back to that page. Did you circle any words? Why or why not? Which of those words would you ascribe to Jesus in your vision of the throne room above? When Bob asked this question at a retreat in Montana, one of the counselors smugly slapped her notebook closed. "None of the words apply because Jesus is not human anymore."

Jesus did not shed humanity as he returned to a heavenly home. He did not come here slumming, only then to go home, sloughing off creaturely dirt like cleaning his boots before coming into the house. Neither did Jesus don latex gloves of humanity to be deposited in the biohazard bin as he finished work.

In Luke 24, Jesus joined the disciples for a meal after his resurrection. They were skeptical that he was actually present with them. "Look at my hands and my feet; see that it is I myself. Touch me and see; for a ghost does not have flesh and bones as you see that I have." Jesus then asked for some fish to eat. The disciples handed over the fish "while in their joy they were disbelieving and still wondering." The scene could be from a Shakespearean comedy!

When we speak of the living Christ, we recognize that the Human Being still lives as the Son of God. We join Paul in confessing, "There is one God; there is also one mediator between God and humankind, Christ Jesus, himself human, who gave himself as ransom for all." There *is* a mediator who *is* human … *now*. Because of Christ's presence on our behalf, God will never look up and ask, "Who let the riff-raff in here?"

Theologian Gerrit Scott Dawson's description presents a thrilling picture of Christ's ascension:

Still wearing our flesh, he passed through the heavens. The principalities and powers were disarmed. He led captivity captive—humanity, long captive to sin and death, rode in his train of glory as he made his way. Then, Jesus entered within the veil, into the Holy of

Holies, the direct presence of God the Father. He entered, Hebrews tells us, as a forerunner for us. He appears there now, wearing our humanity, on our behalf. He is the new and living way to God.

We need not cower before the throne as if scurrying to please a demanding parent, holding our breath that God will tolerate our presence. The reconciling work of Christ satisfies God completely for eternity. Our intricate box-building adds nothing. Christ stands with us as our advocate, our high priest and our brother. We are free to love and be loved by God.

At this juncture, you must maintain a delicate balance. If you imagine a throne room with your arm slung over the Son's shoulders and the two of you giving each other high-five hand slaps, then you make a dangerous mistake. To act with unholy familiarity toward a holy God is profanity. Christ is not your buddy.

A newspaper recently ran an article on Jesus as one of the most lucrative pop icons in our culture. It included pictures of various celebrities wearing T-shirts with "Jesus Is My Homeboy" stretched tightly across ample breasts, humongous glittering crosses adorning rappers' necks, and air-brushed pictures of Jesus' face on birthday cakes. Who could bring themselves to cut the first piece? Leaders of various religious organizations decried the culture's profane use of God.

Ironically and tragically, we Christians teach this profanity. Look around your house. Does the car in your garage sport a faded bumper sticker that says "Honk If You Love Jesus"? Is there a spoon rest on your stove in the shape of a cross and painted with sunflowers? Look on the shelves in your children's rooms. Do you find a precious statue of Jesus playing soccer alongside a young girl or perhaps fishing beside a grandfather and young boy?

We draw cartoons that show Jesus riding in our golf cart. He is portrayed in a business suit as our CEO. We collectively spend millions of dollars hanging slightly smaller versions of the rapper's cross from our ears. Check out the coin bank molded as a shocking-red-flocked ceramic statue of Jesus. It gives a whole new meaning to "Jesus saves," does it not? We dilute the gospel by making Jesus our own personal buddy. We present the Son of God in ways that deny his stature as the God of this universe. What surprises us about the culture around us taking our cue and running with it? We wrongly worship our salvation while profaning our Savior.

Worthy is the Lamb, who was slain, to receive power and wealth and wisdom and strength and honor and glory and praise! ... To him who sits on the throne and to the Lamb be praise and honor and glory and power, for ever and ever! Revelation 5

watch

The Son of God is alive, and we want what he has. We want to be rescued from perishing in the black hole of self-regard. Eternal life that expands without ceasing exists for us now. If John 3:16 matters at all, it will not suffice to hold our breath for the entirety of our life on this earth, just praying we can last until we make it to heaven.

As we both approach our big FIVE-O birthdays, the "shall not perish" part of John 3:16 weighs on us more each day. We hear the promise of eternal life, but someone neglected to tell our bodies. Perhaps you join us in that your rear end is not where or what it used to be. Maybe you need reading glasses to see these words. You perceive yourself to be a marathon runner. Your ankles, however, only want to run a mile.

We still grieve over graves and want to jump in the hole after the casket. We whisper wistfully of loved ones we have "lost." This temporal experience of perishing happens both slowly and suddenly. As a people of resurrection, we cling to the promise that there has been and will be victory over death. Theologian Philip Yancey wrote that "Jesus underscored the central message of the Bible, that life consists in more than the years we spend on earth, and reality consists in more than we can see with telescopes and microscopes."

Christ, fully human and fully divine, stands in the triune Godhead, in the service of God's love, living eternal life, clothed with honor and dignity and glory. Christ projects this future back to humanity in the present through the Holy Spirit, marking the place of eternity in the now.

> Expansive life allows the hope of the future
> to erupt into the possibility of today.

• • • • • a story from Joni

I knelt on the floor in the bathroom, bending over my elderly mother's gnarled and tough toenails. Bluish bruises evidenced Mom's refusal to wear shoes as she did her yard work. Her multiple sclerosis is enough of a prison without confining those prancing toes as the ultimate insult. I picked out an electric red polish to pretty things up a bit.

A moment of quiet hovered as I began gliding the brush over the toenails. An unspoken sadness hung in the silence like humidity. Those toes had danced a thousand miles. They had twirled to music under crystal chandeliers and even under God's own starry sky. Now, on their best days, Mom's feet take her through only the most basic activities. On their worst days, they lie in bed attached to immobile legs.

The sun spilled over us through the bathroom window. I had a visceral feeling of God's presence as more than I could see. What looked like slow death already folded into eternal life. The dark of night intermingled with the dawn of day. I smiled at Mom's sassy red nails. I suspected God liked the color we had chosen.

• • • • •

At Communion
by Madeleine L'Engle

Whether I kneel or stand or sit in prayer
I am not caught in time nor held in space,
But, thrust beyond this posture, I am where
Time and eternity are face to face;
Infinity and space meet in this place
Where crossbar and upright hold the One
In agony and in all Love's embrace.
The power in helplessness which was begun
When all the brilliance of the flaming sun
Contained itself in the small confines of a child
Now comes to me in this strange action done
In mystery. Break time, break space, O wild
And lovely power. Break me; thus am I dead,
Am resurrected now in wine and bread.

Through Christ, we experience a world with multiple dimensions. We hold dual passports in heaven and earth. Tertullian, an early church theologian, wrote, "The way of ascent was thereafter leveled with the ground, by the footsteps of the Lord, and an entrance thereafter opened up by the might of Christ." Innovative pastor and activist Brian McLaren spoke of this leveling as a "truly creative tension":

> The kingdom of this world has become the kingdom of our Lord and of his Christ, his Messiah, his liberating King. The world has not yet become the kingdom, and yet we see that it has. It is in that tension—perhaps the most truly creative tension in the world—that the secret message of Jesus dances, glimmers, shines, and calls us to live: seeing the kingdom here, and seeking and praying for it to come.

It is a mystery and a paradox. We live in a Kingdom that is now and is yet to be, ripe with possibilities. How does that affect your next breath? It gives you freedom from death as the ultimate reality. Life on this earth has space to be what it is, no more and no less. Bonhoeffer said we do not have to "demand eternities" from this life. We can accept the dichotomies of pain and joy, good and bad, and the transcendent and the mundane without trying to wring perfection out of each minute. We can give this life space to breathe. It speaks neither the only nor the last word.

Christ does not ask us for a minimalist participation in his kingdom. He calls for a radical love of God and of other human beings. Listen to the master of analogy, Frederick Buechner, comparing Jesus to the Mad Hatter:

> The world says, Mind your own business, and Jesus says, There is no such thing as your own business. The world says, Follow the wisest course and be a success, and Jesus says, Follow me and be crucified. The world says, Drive carefully—the life you save may be your own—

and Jesus says, Whoever would save his life will lose it, and whoever loses his life for my sake will find it. The world says, Law and order, and Jesus says, Love. The world says, *get*, and Jesus says, *give*. In terms of the world's sanity, Jesus is crazy as a coot, and anybody who thinks he can follow him without being a little crazy too is laboring less under a cross than under a delusion.

Love God with your whole being and love others as you love yourself. These two simple statements, which Jesus called the greatest commandments, have cataclysmic effects if taken seriously.

McLaren described the effect of our settling for lesser loves: "We have been preoccupied with guilt and money, power and fear, control and status—not with service and love, justice and mercy, humility and hope. Frankly, our music has too often been shallow, discordant, or played with a wooden concern for technical correctness but without feeling and passion. Or it has been played with passion but has departed from the true notes, rhythm, and harmonies of the Master."

> You are a letter from Christ,
> written not with ink
> but with the Spirit of the living God,
> not on tablets of stone
> but on tablets of human hearts.
>
> 2 Corinthians 3

The Spirit of God writes Christ on human hearts as we obey the law of love. This kind of obedience will shake up the status quo. It takes life that was turned upside down by death and flips it to life lived right side up.

Love your enemies, lend to those in need, weep with those who weep, do good to all, bless each other, pray with each other, expect nothing in return, show mercy, do not judge, do not condemn, pardon freely, give an offender the other cheek or your only coat in the middle of a snowstorm. In this, we follow the crucified God. Jürgen Moltmann, who came to faith while in a prisoner-of-war camp, saw such sacrificial love as the signature of Christ:

> When the crucified Jesus is called the "image of the invisible God," the meaning is that *this* is God, and God is like *this*. God is not greater than he is in this humiliation. God is not more glorious than he is in this self-surrender. God is not more powerful than he is in this helplessness. God is not more divine than he is in this humanity.... *Here he himself is love with all his being.*

We manifest the grace of God through Christ by the power of the Holy Spirit. As Christ "is love with all his being," so are we to be such love. In loving well, we bring an aroma of possibility and hope. We fulfill our fully human purpose to glorify God as love shines from God through us and out into the world.

wait

The end of Luke's narrative on the life of Christ tells of the disciples following the resurrected Son out of the city. There Christ lifted up his hands to bless the disciples and "while He was blessing them, He parted from them." Christ then ascended into heaven. Can you fathom what it felt like to be left on the ground? How long did the disciples stand there shielding their eyes from the sun as they gazed upward in confusion?

Christ promised we would not be left as orphans. God sent the Holy Spirit as an Advocate in the Son's absence. Jesus said in John 14, "The Advocate, the Holy Spirit, whom the Father will send in my name, will teach you all things and will remind you of everything I have said to you." This Advocate is the subject of our next chapter. The Spirit testifies to the truth of Christ and guarantees the future promise of our resurrection, giving a fore-taste of heaven that keeps us sane.

On our very best days, when everything and everyone is go-ing our way, this world will still not be enough to satisfy our deepest longings. We have a memory of hearing holy footsteps in a garden each evening. Scale a high mountaintop or linger on a deserted sandy beach. Let the wind blow across the skin of your face. If you listen carefully with your whole being, you might hear an echo of what was and what will someday be again. Ancient saints call these moments thin places—in one move, you could reach through the veil and touch heaven.

Jesus promised to come back for us. "I go to prepare a place for you ... and I will come again ... so that where I am, there you may be also." Some days Jesus' absence breeds doubt and fear. Other days we clearly hear the Spirit of God's testimony, and our faith is great.

We wait like band roadies milling at the gate, restless for a rock star to come into view. We lean out our windows and gaze at the sky. Our eyes peer intently in hopes of being the first to see Jesus. Sometimes we imagine that cloud formations look like the face of Jesus—as if we know what his face looks like, as if Jesus hides in the clouds. Call it desperation on our part. Our ears strain to hear the faint echo of trumpet blasts announc-ing Jesus' return. We wait. For where Jesus is, we want to be.

Buechner understood the yearning: "His very absence here in the dust speaks of his presence. Our very brokenness here speaks of wholeness and holiness. The emptiness we carry around inside us through the dust whispers like a seashell of the great sea that it belongs to and that belongs to it."

The living God adopts us as children of the Light. While we glimpse God's glory this side of heaven, we will not be truly home until we stand in the presence of our Redeemer. Christ is both our destination and our way. Often the most rigorous spiritual discipline is to tarry in the present instead of wishing it away.

Lord of the Dance
by Jennifer Lynn Woodruff

He was the Word, a wild and dancing Word,
before the world began; he danced in flame,
and galaxies were born, and songs became
the sinew of our bones, and he was Lord.

He danced in bread and wine, and in the bright
blue fountains of the Water of our birth,
and all the bells rang, and along the earth
the incense of a prayer rose, fresh and light.

He danced in speech, in names that had a power,
in dreams with symbols vibrant and unknown,
and all that was and is and is to come
was whole in grace and worship in that hour.

But we have fenced him in and tied him down;
we think he comes as words and not as Word,
as only what we prove, what we have heard—
not seen, not tasted, and therefore not found.

We preach a thousand sermons, and we lift
a thousand prayers in motions memorized,
and stumble home and have not realized:
the dance is mind and heart—the dance is gift.

He seeks us in the bread we fear to break,
the banners that we lift with trembling hand,
the images we fail to understand,
the steps in God's strange dance we fear to take.

He is the Word, a wild and dancing Word;
he sings; his joy is fierce, his longing deep.
He calls us from ourselves and bids us weep
and dance and worship him, for he is Lord.

LifeSpace

chapter four

BRE

ATH

ENERGY

AIR

BREATH

Now the earth
was without shape
and empty,
and darkness was
over the surface

RUSH

of the watery deep,

LIFE

but the Spirit of God
was moving
over the surface
of the water.

WHISPER

WIND

MOTION

The Spirit of God—the Hebrew *ruach*, the mighty wind—hovers, swirls, broods over the primordial deep at the genesis of life. God begins to speak and sets the world in motion. "Let there be light. Let there be sky. Let there be earth. Let there be heavens." God reaches down into the dust of the ground and forms the human. Still flaccid nostrils fill with oxygen, and a living being rises up. The breath of Life, pure elixir, rushes in with generative power.

By God's pleasure, we live on borrowed air. The Holy Spirit, third person of the triune God, threads into and through our lives without delineation between our breath and the Breath.

> When you take away their breath,
> they die and return to their dust.
> When you send forth your Breath,
> they are created.
>
> Psalm 104

The possibility of Life suffuses our days as our being is inextricably tethered to the Eternally Living One. Yet we settle. We settle for tiny snippets of air: little molecules drawn through pursed lips and barely taken past our throats. Our chests have long forgotten the God-sized onslaught of Life that came as our lungs unfolded in a first birthing cry. Shallow sighs too easily satisfy.

• • • • • a story from Bob

Our families volunteer at a camp for people with disabilities each summer. The camp provides a crucial respite for those who live in the nether lands as exceptions to the able-bodied rule. The days at camp fill with much hilarity and high jinks. Palsied hands flip over ice-cream bowls at random and clown outfits are the uniform of choice.

Jennifer, a longtime camper, celebrated her eighteenth birthday this year. A childhood accident on a playground left her a quadriplegic. *Jennifer's wheelchair resembles a spaceship: signals and lights trill and blink. The most important signal monitors a ventilator pushing air in and out of Jennifer's lungs day and night. Her "vent" is literally her life. A scant few minutes without it would bring brain damage and then death.*

The campers love riding horses, with Jennifer always one of the first in line to take a turn. Imagine this scene: Jennifer motors across the grounds and up to the stables in her chair. Her family trails behind. Her mother unbuckles Jennifer's safety straps and prepares to disconnect the vent. A staff person stands waiting on a wooden picnic table next to the horse. The mother unplugs the lifeline. Several men lift Jennifer up into the arms of the person on the table, who then gingerly transfers her onto the horse. The whole process happens with swift precision. I hold my breath.

Angie, a woman who has worked at the camp for years, waits astride the horse. She loves to ride with Jennifer. Angie immediately attaches a green ventilation bag to the hole in Jennifer's throat. She uses her hand to pump the bag in and out as the horse slowly saunters down the path. Jennifer and Angie beam with smiles of success. The crowd claps. Tears flow.

Angie pumps. Jennifer breathes.
Angie pumps. Jennifer breathes.

Angie and everyone in the scene are instruments of God's Spirit. Breath expands from the constricting confines of the chair to the joyful ride on the horse to the gentle summer breeze in the trees and beyond. I imagine Angie's breathing quickly synchronizes with Jennifer's, each chest moving in tandem to a gracious rhythm of life.

When I think of the person of the Spirit as the essence of life, Jennifer's face appears. She understands breath and life. None of us has a guarantee of one more breath. Only by God's grace do our lungs fill with air and then expel that air to fill again.

000316663212

Sell your books at
sellbackyourBook.com!
Go to sellbackyourBook.com
and get an instant price quote.
We even pay the shipping - see
what your old books are worth
today!

In this second-by-second demonstration of sustaining power,
God's glory shines.

● ● ● ● ●

Spirit of the living God, fall fresh on me.
Spirit of the living God, fall fresh on me.

The Holy Spirit moves in human history through the initial and ongoing animation of human life. Old Testament prophets and leaders received a special anointing by the Spirit. God directed Moses to gather seventy elders for such a calling: "I will take some of the Spirit that is on you and put it on them; and they shall bear the burden of the people along with you so that you will not bear it all by yourself."

The prophet Joel anticipated a day when the Holy Spirit would anoint not simply a few, but all God's people. "I will pour out my spirit on all flesh; your sons and daughters shall prophesy, your old men shall dream dreams, and your young men shall see visions. Even on the male and female slaves, in those days, I will pour out my spirit." Peter proclaimed the fulfillment of this promise when Christ's followers were baptized with the Spirit at Pentecost.

Having opened the way to eternal life, Christ foretold of his impending departure in John 14. Christ anticipated the Spirit coming in his absence. "And I will ask the Father, and he will give you another Advocate, to be with you forever. This is the Spirit of truth, whom the world cannot receive, because it neither sees him nor knows him. You know him, because he abides with you and he will be in you." With Christ as the portal to the reality beyond ourselves, the Holy Spirit provides ongoing testimony to what is really real.

A woman came to the well with a jar
and left with a river.

Isaiah likened the presence of the Holy Spirit to water poured out on a thirsty land. Similarly, Jesus offered the Spirit as living water in John 7: "Let anyone who is thirsty come to me, and let the one who believes in me drink. As the scripture has said, 'Out of the believer's heart shall flow rivers of living water.' Now he said this about the Spirit, which believers in him were to receive."

The transforming power of the Spirit as living water is seen in 2 Corinthians 3. "And all of us, with unveiled faces, seeing the glory of the Lord as though reflected in a mirror, are being transformed into the same image from one degree of glory to another; for this comes from the Lord, the Spirit." Our journey toward fulfilling our fully human purpose encompasses this transformative process.

The Spirit is unpredictable, unrestrained, persistent and powerful.

Mystery surrounds the person of the Spirit. The Western mind has a hard time grappling with the concept. To us, mystery merely represents a dearth of data to be cured by uncovering all the facts. A puzzle that can be completed as long as all the pieces are in the box. A spy novel that tantalizes with clues but eventually reveals the answer in the final chapter. A magician concealing a spring-loaded bouquet of fake flowers up her sleeve. The magic may stump the children, but we adults have it figured out. Everything can eventually be known or solved.

The Spirit of God does not traffic in our pitiful constructions of mystery, nimbly avoiding our shameless attempts to grasp for control. The Spirit is unpredictable, unrestrainable, persistent and powerful. In John 3, we see the Greek *pneuma* used for both the Holy Spirit and the wind. "The wind blows where it chooses, and you hear the sound of it, but you do not know where it comes from or where it goes. So it is with everyone who is born of the Spirit."

This picture of the Holy Spirit cannot be thwarted by indifference or contained in a box. The wind swirls through and around and over and under our masking tape lines without a care. Common caricatures of God's Spirit tend to minimize this mysterious power.

Battery Pack

The Spirit acts like a power pack for obedience. Turn the Spirit on or off—your choice. Switch on, you obey. Switch off, who knows what could happen.

Vending Machine

The Spirit gives you what you want if you make the right moves. Sometimes you get a surprise. You pretend you wanted it.

Referee

The Spirit blows the whistle when you step out of bounds. You choose whether to stay in or out. No instant replays can reverse the calls.

Scoutmaster

The Spirit tells you where to go. Use the compass correctly, find your way home and get an Eagle Scout badge.

Friendly Ghost

The Spirit is a friendly ghost, some ethereal being lingering at your shoulder. The Spirit only gives treats, not tricks, dispensing gifts like candy.

Some people grope for a particular event that heralds the coming of the Spirit in their lives. They seek mountaintop experiences or an incantation of perfect words in a particular prayer or formula to summon God. Surely the Holy Spirit does not inhabit our mundane, daily life, so there must be a unique way to access the power.

• • • • • stop a moment

Glance back over the pictures above. Do any of them fit your view of the Holy Spirit's role in your life? If so, how did you come to that view? If not, what image would you use? Do you leave room for the mystery of the Spirit's work? Do you believe in the personal being of the Spirit of God who seeks relationship with you?

• • • • •

None of the caricatures provide for transformation. They demonstrate a small and myopic understanding of the Spirit. While the depictions above bear some truth, none of them envision the fully human life as an existence that reflects the knowledge of God and trust in God through an expansive experience of living.

We do not solve the mystery of life with God.
We LIVE the mystery of life with God.

The mystery of the Spirit of God working in our lives brings fear and trepidation for many of us. Safer to have a small God you can control than a big God who refuses to be boxed or ignored. Safer to think rebellion will be overlooked. We settle for life in black and white when God offers life in technicolor. The Spirit witnesses to the truth of the gospel that under girds our lives with possibility. Paul saw that "to set the mind on the flesh is death, but to set the mind on the Spirit is life and peace."

The Spirit of God ...
  Reminds us of our worth as image bearers of God.
  Testifies to our identity anchored in Christ.
  Enlarges our view of a greater reality.
  Transforms our affections for God and others.

The Spirit does not promise to align our circumstances with our expectations. The truth of the gospel—Christ conquered death and offers life—means that we are people of beginnings. God's mercies dawn new every morning. We celebrate mystery in the timing of God's movement in our lives, in God's grace that lavishly sustains us and in the testimony of who God is despite circumstances that bring traces or watersheds of doubt.

Novelist L. M. Montgomery gave insight into this realm of possibility through a young girl's eyes in *Emily of New Moon*:

It had always seemed to Emily, ever since she could remember, that she was very, very near to a world of wonderful beauty. Between it and herself hung only a thin curtain; she could never draw the curtain aside—but sometimes, just for a moment, a wind fluttered it and then it was as if she caught a glimpse of the enchanting realm beyond—only a glimpse—and heard a note of unearthly music....And always when the flash came to her Emily felt life was a wonderful, mysterious thing of persistent beauty.

God's good pleasure draws the curtain aside. The moments cannot be summoned or contrived.

A fragrant magnolia blossom sits in your grandmother's crystal bowl. The sunlight slants through the window just so. Your eye catches a glance of blinding white as the sun captures the flower. The crystal refracts the beam of light to splash a rainbow of color onto the tablecloth. The moment mesmerizes. You stand perfectly still, arrested in time. And so the Spirit of God moves.

The transforming work of the Holy Spirit breaks through the medium of this world. Barbara Brown Taylor asked, "Do we still believe in a God who blows through closed doors and sets our heads on fire? . . . Or have we come to an unspoken agreement that our God is pretty old and tired by now, someone to whom we may address our prayer requests but not anyone we really expect to change our lives?"

Do you believe God can and does transform human beings? We are not talking about getting a homeless person to a shelter for a meal and a hot shower to shine him up. Nor being able to arrange your face into a beaming smile at the grocery store when your home life is pure hell. Neither are we talking about a little tweaking here and there: a little more patience with the kids or a nicer tone with your sister.

Do you make comments like, "Well, that is just the way I am." Or "She'll never change." Or "I've known him all his life and he will *never* _____." You fill in the blank. There is more than we will ever know. More room for growth. More space to be. More God to love. Our potential to be fully human does not start with just the way we are but with just the way God is. In this alone we find air to breathe.

Transformation results in living beyond yourself through a metamorphosis of being. The work of the Spirit begins now and never ceases. As Paul wrote to Titus, "When the goodness and loving kindness of God our Savior appeared, he saved us, not because of any works of righteousness that we had done, but according to his mercy, through the water of rebirth and renewal by the Holy Spirit." Rebirth and renewal connote a permanent change in circumstance. An advanced course in box-building will not help you.

Robert Jenson connected the power of conversion to the good news of the gospel. If someone comes to confess cheating and coveting, you might say, "In the name of Jesus our Lord, you are forgiven." Jenson noted, "This utterance *is* a conversion of the penitent's life, from a situation in which the word he or she hears and must live by is 'You are a cheat and a coveter,' to one in which the word he or she hears and must live by is 'You are Jesus' beloved.'" The words you live by change.

In Ephesians 1, Paul spoke of the Holy Spirit as the One who marks this conversion in our lives. The seal of the Holy Spirit speaks to the ongoing work of transformation. Our hearts' affection changes such that our gaze turns to the glorious person of God: "In him [Christ] you also, when you had heard the word of truth, the gospel of your salvation, and had believed in him, were marked with the seal of the promised Holy Spirit; this is the pledge of our inheritance toward redemption as God's own people, to the praise of his glory."

> Spirit of the living God, fall fresh on me.
> Spirit of the living God, fall fresh on me.

Our dear friend, the late theologian Stanley Grenz, described the Spirit of God placing us in the dynamic of the Trinitarian love. We stand "as co-heirs with Christ of the treasure—the love and the name—that the Father eternally lavishes on his Son." In Romans 5, Paul recognized the hope residing in this love: "Hope does not disappoint us, because God's love has been poured into our hearts through the Holy Spirit that has been given to us."

It has been over a month since you last spoke. You said and he said and you said and he said. Then there was nothing else to say. The words hung out there like arrows, piercing and prickly. Now you see him across the aisle at the bookstore. The easiest route makes a sharp left through the cooking section and avoids him completely. You hide behind the self-help books while making a decision. What does it look like to choose life right now? With a longing glance to the left, you step across the aisle and tap your friend on the shoulder. And so the Spirit of God moves.

The anchor of God's love allows a bold and fearless embrace of human relationships. Free to be authentic and real, we explore the way of grace, mercy, compassion, forgiveness, peace and faithfulness. The Spirit transforms us over and over, from glory to glory, without ceasing.

Your son steps up to bat in the baseball game. The field glimmers Scotland green with lines chalked straight and narrow. The man-boy's arms ripple as they move to swing. A wafting breeze stirs the faint whisper of your father's voice inside you. His memory sits close on the metal bleacher. Everything outside the baseball fence had been a battleground for the two of you. Only the magic of innings played on fresh-cut grass brought peace. Long ago, you heard your father's love as he yelled, "Go, Son, Go!" Your eyes now follow your son around the bases. "Go, Son, Go!" you scream. Under your breath you whisper words you once craved to hear, "I love you." And so the Spirit of God moves.

This life, superintended by the Holy Spirit—the Unseen One—juxtaposes multiple layers of reality. There is so much more than we see with our eyes. Eternity slips through the thin curtain to dazzle us into worship. The mystic Maggie Ross wrote of subverting "our perceptions of time and space in order to plunge us to the great stillness at the heart of things," to make space for beholding our dwelling place of eternity.

• • • • • a story from Joni

Doli came several days late to our teaching in Rwanda. She and her husband traveled overland from the Republic of Congo. They arrived weary and covered with dust. At forty years old, Doli neared the end of her fourteenth full-term pregnancy. Only six children still live. The last child has severe disabilities and depends completely on Doli's care.

Doli's huge brown eyes followed our every move as we taught, switching between us and the interpreter. I wanted to know her story, but the language barrier seemed impassable. We smiled at each other constantly to bridge the gap.

One evening, Doli and I pulled up three chairs, asking the interpreter to join us. Within minutes we bridged the physical space between us. Hands joined and bodies leaned close together. We did not have weeks or months or years to know each other. That night had to suffice. Words were not our friend as we lurched between two languages. It did not matter. The Spirit of God hovered over two mothers of two colors from two continents who met as sisters under the starry sky.

I will probably never see Doli again this side of heaven. I have a photograph of her face peering from behind a sphere like the one we introduce in the first chapter. Doli's eyes pierce my heart. I envision the Spirit's sustaining breath moving between us. We were at the great stillness together, peering through the curtain, beholding eternity from wobbly plastic chairs in the dirt of Rwanda.

• • • • •

We exist to behold. Behold, God is coming in the clouds! Behold, the Lamb of God! Behold, the Lion of Judah! Behold, I bring you glad tidings! Behold, I show you a mystery! Behold, the tabernacle of God is within you! Behold, lift up your eyes! The great I AM moves about this world with or without our consent. Created as instruments of response to God's great drama, we must pay attention.

Poet Gerard Manley Hopkins expressed awe at the presence of God's Spirit in our world:

> There lives the dearest freshness deep down things;
> And though the last lights off the black West went
> Oh, morning, at the brown brink eastward, springs—
> Because the Holy Ghost over the bent
> World broods with warm breast and with ah! bright wings.

Quoting this poem, Frederick Buechner encouraged our response to the Spirit. "It is our business, as we journey, to keep our hearts open to that, to the bright-winged presence of the Holy Ghost within us and the Kingdom of God among us." Our next chapter, "Shift," explores that journey of open hearts turned to gaze on God.

Take a moment to practice breathing. Fill your chest. Let the air seep down to the bottom of your lungs. Push all the air back out and then take air in again. As you slowly inhale and exhale, say a prayer of thanksgiving for the Spirit of Life. Be still and know God in the very next breath you take.

Ada judged she had lived a good life—
a strenuous one and a lucky one. For she had
truly felt God's power.... She buried two fine
husbands. It was not everybody got so deep into
the battering and jabbing of it all, got in the path
of the great God's might. She moved across the
burning plains, crossed two mountain ranges.
She saw from the western shore with her own
eyes the mild islands rolling off in the light, the
way they must have looked at the foundation
of the world....

She felt her freedom. Reared two boys to
manhood, busted open this wilderness by the
sea, buried the men on their lands. She saw a
white horse roll in wild strawberries and stand
up red. She took part in the great drama. It had
been her privilege to peer into the deepest well
hole of life's surprise. She felt the fire of God's
wild breath on her face.

Annie Dillard

LifeSpace

chapter five

IFT

Each morning and evening, Jewish families offer a traditional prayer in households and synagogues throughout the world. Words are sung in an ancient, liturgical rhythm, reverberating off stone ceilings or whispered stealthily to avoid attention. The prayer from Old Testament scripture—the shema—begins.

Hear, O Israel: The Lord is our God, the Lord alone. You shall love the Lord your God with all your heart, and with all your soul, and with all your might. Keep these words that I am commanding you today in your heart. Recite them to your children and talk about them when you are at home and when you are away, when you lie down and when you rise. Bind them as a sign on your hand, fix them as an emblem on your forehead, and write them on the doorposts of your house and on your gates.

The prayer acknowledges love for God as the center of being. It lifts up the gaze of the people. Hear the truth, O people. The Lord is God. Hear the truth, O people. The love of God is our portion and our life.

We often turn the great *shema* on its head. We live life topsyturvy like a child on a swing, head thrown back with our eyes beneath our chins, dizzied by the view as we go forward and back. Or like novice kayakers who have flipped in roaring rapids, barreling down the river with our helmets underwater, communing with the fishes. We struggle for breath.

Life upside down comes from forsaking God as our first love. False promises of transcendence and satisfaction seduce us. Our focus shifts away from the beauty of God. Sideward glances lead to slow suffocation in our own folly. As suggested by C. S. Lewis, we are far too easily pleased.

There is hope. The Spirit of God moves in our lives to reorient our affection to its true north. The work of resurrection, begun in Christ and guided by the Spirit, flips the kayak right side up, and we are gulping air once again.

Through this reorientation, the fully human life is realized as an existence that reflects the knowledge of God and trust in God through an expansive experience of living. Indifference to God, outright rebellion against God and the performance art of box-building result in life with a lower case *l*. We have no idea what we are missing. The first chapter, "Gaze," uses the visual of the sphere to suggest a life that moves ever outward into the fullness of God's glory.

"Dirt," the second chapter, rejects the idea that humanity is a problem needing solution. Instead, we celebrate our fully human purpose to glorify God and enjoy God forever. In the third chapter, "Way," we see the affirmation of humanity by the incarnation of God. God the Son came to be Emmanuel, "God with us," joining us as dirt in the dirt. Christ remains fully human and fully divine, drawing us as followers into a reality beyond ourselves.

The fully human **life** is an expansive experience of **living**

We straddle this world and the next. The previous chapter, "Breath," reveals the person of the Holy Spirit who animates our lives by transforming our affection for God.

With that framework in place, we now turn to the central question as we practice this life with God. Some ask, "How do I stay inside the lines?" or "How can I be good enough for God to love me?" Sam in Manhattan wonders, "Can 'things are fine' be enough? Can I get all I need in 'fine'?" The rebellious Israelites asked, "What is God doing for me today?" Their memory of God's provision lasted about twenty-four hours. The central question comes down to this:

What do you love?

Is the *shema* the guiding orientation of your days or are you running this river upside down? In Psalm 73, a radical centering on God occurs: "Whom have I in heaven but you? And there is nothing on earth that I desire other than you. My flesh and my heart may fail, but God is the strength of my heart and my portion forever." To love the real God requires unleashing a holy passion for all that is lovely. What do you desire in place of God? Maybe comfort, stability, affection, opportunity, piety or a promotion at your job? What *do* you love?

The Old Testament prophet Jonah provides a classic example of misguided love. God directed him to head to Ninevah. Wickedness reigned in the city, and God had a few words to say about it. Jonah was understandably reluctant to go. He expected his head to be delivered on a stick. After a minor detour through the belly of a whale, Jonah ended up wandering the streets of Ninevah, warning of the coming judgment of God: "Forty days more, and Nineveh shall be overthrown!" Imagine him wearing a sandwich board hand-lettered with this dire pronouncement.

The Bible makes a simple statement: "The people of Ninevah believed God." Good move on their part. The people began fasting and covering themselves with sackcloth, crying out for mercy. "Who knows? God may relent and change his mind; he may turn from his fierce anger, so that we do not perish." The people turned toward God, and the divine wrath turned aside.

Now back to Jonah with the sandwich board. The outcome incensed him. How dare God love those people like that! "That is why I fled to Tarshish at the beginning; for I knew that you are a gracious God and merciful, slow to anger, and abounding in steadfast love, and ready to relent from punishing. And now, O LORD, please take my life from me, for it is better for me to die than to live."

You would expect Jonah to celebrate the salvation of an entire city of people. After all, that was the point of his calling.

The Ninevites held their breath, hoping for mercy. "Who knows?" Jonah *knew* God to be love. He himself had experienced that love during his own rebellion against God. Yet self-interest raised its ugly head in the face of God's mercy for others. Pride took over. Jonah's turn inward will make his wish come true: death instead of life.

In Mark 12, Jesus fielded a query from a Jewish scribe: "Which commandment is the first of all?" Jesus answered with words his wily opponent knew by heart: "Hear, O Israel: the Lord our God, the Lord is one; you shall love the Lord your God with all your heart, and with all your soul, and with all your mind, and with all your strength. The second is this, You shall love your neighbor as yourself." Jesus' response to the scribe follows the *shema* of old. It reflects a vertical love from the creature for the Creator and a horizontal love for others.

To love God for God's own sake means the perfections of God bring us the greatest joy. Seeing God's glory manifested in Ninevah, where forgiveness and mercy turned away wrath, should have sent Jonah dancing in the streets. Jonah delivered God's message with his mouth, but prideful anger revealed the misguided affection of Jonah's heart.

Faithfulness, longsuffering, mercy, compassion, kindness, attention, grace, sacrifice and forgiveness mark the character of the God we love. As image-bearers, we are called to celebrate those perfections and, in turn, manifest them in our love for others.

What do you love?

Reformer Martin Luther wrote of impure and perverted lovers who "seek their own advantage in God, neither love nor praise His bare goodness, but have an eye to themselves and consider only how good God is to them, that is, how deeply He makes them feel His goodness and how many good things He does to them ...They delight in their salvation much more than their Savior, in the gift more than the Giver, in the creature rather than in the Creator."

Salvation more than Savior
Gift more than Giver
Creature more than Creator

We often invert our created purpose by turning the spotlight on ourselves. We wrongly presume that Jesus Christ, Lord of all, is captivated with us, prizing us above all others to die for us. Look at this chorus from an old hymn:

> How marvelous, how wonderful!
> And my song shall ever be!
> How marvelous, how wonderful!
> Is my Savior's love for me!

It *is* indeed marvelous that the Savior loves us. But the preeminent praise belongs to the Savior and the perfection of God's gracious love. God's grace toward humans does not exalt *us*; it exalts *God*. Without the righteousness of Christ credited to us, we are bankrupt.

The inversion from love of God to love of self looks like a wood shaving, curling into a tight spring at its center. This suicidal turn leads us away from joy. Selfishly, we really love God's gifts, even when we profess to love God. Luther called this using God rather than enjoying God. This incurvature of the soul is the marrow of sin.

The vortex of selfish love acts like a black hole in space. A star reaches the end of its life, leaving a burned-out remnant of matter. That remnant collapses in on itself. It becomes infinitely dense. The path of light rays emitted from the star bend inward and start wrapping around the star itself. Eventually no light escapes, thus the label "black hole." Think about it. The star essentially crushes itself to death.

Shifting our gaze away from God follows the same course. Only a remnant of life remains. Cut off from the expansive source, we turn toward emptiness. The early African theologian Augustine of Hippo wrote of this shift:

> To be sure, man did not fall away from his nature so completely as to lose all being. When he turned towards himself, however, his being became less complete than when he clung to Him Who exists supremely. Thus, to forsake God and to exist in oneself—that is, to be pleased with oneself—is not immediately to lose all being; but it is to come closer to nothingness.

Like water swirling down a drain, life dissipates. Setting our created purpose aside, we move from being human to being creature. We concede life in its excellent enlargedness to trifling existence. John Piper asked the central question of this chapter another way: "God remains gloriously all-satisfying. The human heart remains a ceaseless factory of desires. Sin remains powerfully and suicidally appealing. The battle remains: Where will we drink? Where will we feast?"

What do you love?

Remember looking through a kaleidoscope? You hold the tube up to the light and begin turning the cylinder. Your eyes feast on an explosion of color and design as the crystals shift and tumble. Or have you seen the cool toy eye glasses that refract light into brilliant rays of color? They are disco groovy. You see the world in a wholly new way.

The Spirit of God introduces life in a myriad of hues, making our turn toward the self look drab and monochrome. Community is more beautiful than independence. Forgiveness is more beautiful than revenge. Remembering your anniversary is more beautiful than a litany of excuses for inattention. The kaleidoscope of Life draws our eyes up and out. We do not muster love for God—putting our shoulder to the plow and our nose to the grindstone. We see the person of God with eyes trained for beauty.

If you have a kaleidoscope, rustle it up and put it next to your sphere. If not, keep your eyes peeled for one when you are out and about. Kaleidoscopes make great presents. Get one for yourself!

● ● ● ● ●

Becoming fully human requires a radical shift of gaze that reorients our affection. The Holy Spirit works to flip or invert our self-absorption into an eternal encounter with the divine reality. Augustine experienced a passionate revelation of the person of God:

> You called and cried out loud and shattered my deafness. You were radiant and resplendent, you put to flight my blindness. You were fragrant, and I drew in my breath and now pant after you. I tasted you, and I feel but hunger and thirst for you. You touched me, and I am set on fire to attain the peace which is yours.

LOVE
OF
GOD

We live right side up when the love of God truly becomes our *shema*. The drain transforms into a fountain, fed by the wellspring of Living Water. Jesus' words become a reality: "Those who find their life will lose it, and those who lose their life for my sake will find it."

Marva Dawn, who writes about the nature of worship, called our restored affection a royal waste of time. "Worship is idolatry unless it is a total waste of time in earthly terms, a total immersion in the eternity of God's infinite splendor for the sole purpose of honoring God." Can you be a fool for love?

• • • • • a story from Bob

As a professor in theology, my overriding professional goal for years was to have the right opinion. This aligned with my overriding personal goal, which was to do the right thing. Effective teaching meant helping someone else have the right opinion and do the right thing. I certainly knew the priority of the love of God. I had those scriptures memorized. For me that knowledge translated into a practice of, well, being right. I now thank God for not leaving me to myself. My own self-righteousness was the sin of self-indulgence masked as theological rigor.

My purpose as a human being, let alone a minister of the gospel, is to glorify God and enjoy God forever. Being right means giving the Spirit access to transform my heart's affection, with the law of love as my standard. I am now much more interested in theology as a living conversation about life with God.

Sure, I can still hold my own in a debate. But my taste for such pastimes wanes. So much better to meet you for an iced tea on a sweltering Texas day and to hear how God has moved in you. Tell me your stories of delight so that our hearts may be refreshed.

• • • • •

Paul portrays love right side up perfectly in Colossians 3. "So if you have been raised with Christ, seek the things that are above, where Christ is, seated at the right hand of God. You have stripped off the old self with its practices and have clothed yourselves with the new self, which is being renewed in knowledge according to the image of its creator. Above all, clothe yourselves with love, which binds everything together in perfect harmony."

What do you love?

Spiritual formation has perennially been a topic of great interest. You can get workbooks and videos and programs to take you from Step A to Step Z. Universities offer certification for spiritual directors. Retreat centers entice you with yoga on the side.

We do not have a program for you. If you need five steps or fifty steps, then you had best find another source. Transformation changes the affection of the heart over the course of a lifetime. Remember that simply mustering love for God will not work. "Here. Go love God. Come back when you get it right." No technique or program can produce love for God. The work of the Holy Spirit brings about change for the purpose of God's glory. We seek things that are above, where Christ is. He has what we want.

• • • • • a story from Joni

In the second chapter, I mention my misinformed quest to be a godlet in heaven. The human Joni would hang around on earth until God called me up, like going to the major leagues in baseball. While waiting for the magical switch, I would make, at best, lurching progress here on earth. Hopefully head in a generally forward direction. Detours, switchbacks and poor signage mark the way.

The whole scenario implies I am really just killing time here. Try to be good. Avoid wrong turns. Wait to be snatched out of the muck and mire into a new self in a new place. The Spirit does not truly transform me but simply tries to make me presentable until I get to heaven. I told you I was misinformed!

Eternity for me has already begun. The heavenly realm bursts into this dimension through the incarnated Son. With Christ, I now straddle earth and heaven. The transformation of my affection starts now and continues forever. Some days look better than others down here. The process is the point.

Why does any of this matter? The chorus of one of my favorite country western songs goes, "I'm going to spend my time like it's going out of style ... no matter how much time I buy, I can never spend it all." This life is not about watching the clock tick, biding my time. I am here to spend my days loving God and loving what God loves and how God loves. Eternity happens now. Forget about killing time.

      ●   ●   ●   ●   ●

The process of real, irrevocable change happens in the present as we allow the Spirit of God access to our lives. The fruit of the Spirit's work begins to appear: love, joy, peace, patience, kindness, generosity, faithfulness, gentleness and self-control.

Transformation does not occur in a one-time transaction but in a never-ending process. The Spirit does not replace you with divinity or with another person. The Spirit also does not uncover a good self that hides under your sin. There is no pure heart, imprisoned by the darkness of evil, waiting for the freedom to express itself. Your body is not a culprit while your soul is a saint. Frederick Buechner captured the wide-ranging swath of our sin:

> Let's just suppose that at certain unguarded moments we have it, this inclination to *start* being children of God—have we any idea at all what by the grace of God we are in all likelihood going to have to *stop* being, stop doing, stop having, stop pretending, stop smacking our lips over, stop hating, stop being scared of, stop chasing after till we're blue in the face and sick at the stomach? O God, deliver us from the Lamb of God which taketh away the sin of the world because the sin of the world is our heart's desire, our uniform, our derby hat. O Lamb of God, have mercy on us.

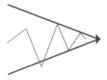

You might have a picture of transformation that looks like the arrows above. You careen against the boundaries of acceptable behavior until you finally get it right. There seems to be an end point of perfection that you will attain. As with an automatic mapping system in your car, you plug in your current location and a desired destination. Soon a voice will say, "You have arrived." Look at the picture. It reeks of smallness and confinement and constriction. Where is God in that?

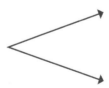

Flipping the arrows, you begin to see the true picture. Get your sphere out and expand it for a multi-dimensional view.

You begin in Christ and move ever outward into the fullness of God's glory. There is freedom to grow, move, breathe. You do not plug in a destination; rather, you allow this life to take on the expansive complexion of God.

• • • • • stop a moment

Take a moment for "Mirror, Mirror, on the wall." We introduce love of self as a drain or black hole, while picturing the love of God as a fountain or wellspring. Let us make this real for you. Think about asking a group of your friends or colleagues or even your family these questions: "Am I a drain or a fountain in your life? Do I give life to you or take life from you? Do I build you up or tear you down?"

What would they say? Do you have the courage to ask someone those questions? You are a drain when you put yourself at the forefront. It takes a lot of fuel to keep that fire burning as you consume the people around you. You are a fountain as the love of God flows through you and splashes onto the people in your life.

Let us try another "Mirror, Mirror, on the wall." When you walk into a room of people, what stance do you take? Do you glide in the door with "Here I am!" waiting for the attention to focus on you? This move can be either loud and boisterous or more subtle by being so shy or awkward that attention comes your way out of sheer pity. Or do you throw open your arms and say, "There you are!" in a gesture of genuine attention toward others? Do you practice flinging love outward?

How do your answers to these questions look in your relationships with others? Does conversation rotate around you, crisis gravitate to you or neediness suck people into your orbit? Or are people buoyed by a blessing of love spilling over them, satiating their thirst? Are you a "Here I am!" person or a "There you are!" person? Are you a drain or a fountain?

● ● ● ● ●

What do you love?

This life with God brings constant change: from death to life, from estrangement to reconciliation, from rebellion to adoration. The Spirit will not force the process upon us. While God invites us to participate in delight, we must "lay ourselves in the way of allurement," as Jonathan Edwards wrote. Our senses open to the movement of the Spirit as we develop a capacity for expansive life in God. As Eugene Peterson writes:

> A shrub in the desert and a tree by the river are both alive, but not quite in the same way: The desert shrub meagerly survives, the watered tree abundantly reproduces.... [There are] conditions which are congenial to developing God-awareness as over against growing God-calluses, looking out for rivers and staying away from deserts. The way we are—the way we spend our money, eat our meals, read a book, treat a stranger—affects our capacity to see the beauty of holiness, hear the word of absolution, feel the touch of love, enter into a life of prayer.

The book pivots with this chapter. Consider rereading it before you move forward. The next several chapters delve further into the practice of life with God as we love what God loves and how God loves. We begin with "Joy" as a delightful celebration of God. Where else would we start? We continue with "Rope" in our commitment to living as a communal family of humanity. In the chapters "Space," "Gift" and "Fool," we explore God's love shining through grace, forgiveness and sacrifice. And "Sight" ties everything back into being fully human with hope in the midst.

JOY remains the ultimate purpose of our transformation. God does not need us to do the work of heaven. God has invited us to the party. We join the psalmist as we pray, "Restore to us the joy of your salvation, and sustain in us a willing spirit." May God incite a passion that consumes our being.

Abbot Lot went to see Abbot Joseph and said:
"Father, according as I am able, I keep my little
rule, and my little fast, my prayer, meditation and
contemplative silence; and according as I am
able I strive to cleanse my heart of bad thoughts:
now what more should I do?" The elder rose up
in reply and stretched out his hands to heaven,
and his fingers became like lamps of fire.
He said: "Why not become all flame?"

The Wisdom of the Desert

chapter six

OY

Is there a single person on whom I can press belief? No sir. All I can do is say, Here's how it went. Here's what I saw. I've been there and am going back. Make of it what you will. Leif Enger

Joy is both a gift and a discipline. The Holy Spirit strips away the God-calluses from your eyes as if removing cataracts. But you can still choose to clench your lids shut and walk around blind.

Growth comes as you train your eyes, nose, ears, skin, tongue—every molecule of your being—to respond to the beauty of God's glory. The Spirit moves in mysterious, subtle ripples over the surface of reality. Are you watching? Do you see? Can you taste the loveliness of God in a fresh fuzzy peach? Enjoy the banging of pots and pans in your mother's kitchen? Appreciate a hilarious story and raucous laughter?

The Holy One pierces the thin curtain. Stay alert. Live chest open, ready to burst into joyous praise at the slightest provocation. The way of allurement awaits you.

Divinity is not playful. The universe was not made in jest but in solemn incomprehensible earnest. By a power that is unfathomably secret, and holy, and fleet. There is nothing to be done about it, but ignore it, or see. Annie Dillard

A dramatic change occurs in the structure of this chapter as we invite you into delight. You will see our stories collected under "signposts" of joy, testifying to the presence of God. Other voices—from poetry, music and the Word—introduce a smorgasbord of images to entice you. King David's psalm of praise for God's goodness threads throughout. Use the signposts to guide you. Practice a royal waste of time in worship; that would be the point, after all.

We wish we could stop by your place and grab you for a hike down a trail. Or perhaps to chant the words of God in melismatic unison. For now, we will have to create our community of delight in the pages of this book. We suggest you circle with a friend and read the chapter aloud. May your appetite for joy in the glorious God increase with each turn of the page.

Here is how it went. Here is what we saw. Make of it what you will.

From Psalm 145. . .

I will exalt you, my God the King;
I will praise your name for ever and ever.
Every day I will praise you
and extol your name forever and ever.
Great is the LORD and most worthy of praise;
his greatness no one can fathom.
One generation commends your works to another;
they tell of your mighty acts.
They speak of the glorious splendor of your majesty—
and I will meditate on your wonderful works.
They tell of the power of your awesome works—
and I will proclaim your great deeds.
They celebrate your abundant goodness
and joyfully sing of your righteousness.

●　　●　　●　　●　　●

Six friends gathered in a Colorado log cabin to talk about God. A perfect elevation for lofty conversation. Joni and I led a discussion on delight and then sent everyone outdoors to commune with God's creation. The aspens sparkled in fall color. The river roared its icy melody. Unfortunately, joy-dampening rain began to fall. We huddled under trees, shivering and peering out through the raindrops. Suddenly the sun broke through the clouds. An astounding triple rainbow spread across the sky, centering

its colorful arc over the cabin. We shouted and pointed.
God showed up in an extravagant swath of glory. **Bob**

 Do you actively seek God through creation? Does the natural world provide an opportunity for delightful discovery, or do you consider a fish bowl on your counter to be sufficient contact with the wild?

Morning Person
by Vassar Miller

God, best at making in the morning, tossed
stars and planets, singing and dancing, rolled
Saturn's rings spinning and humming, twirled the earth
so hard it coughed and spat the moon up, brilliant
bubble floating around it for good, stretched holy
hands till birds in nervous sparks flew forth from
them and beasts—lizards, big and little, apes,
lions, elephants, dogs and cats cavorting,
tumbling over themselves, dizzy with joy when
God made us in the morning too, both man
and woman, leaving Adam no time for
sleep so nimbly was Eve bouncing out of
his side till as night came everything and
everybody, growing tired, declined, sat
down in one soft descended Hallelujah.

•   •   •   •   ●

My run from the ranch house winds down the rutted lane, past
the gate and out into the pasture. I run slowly at first. The speed
increases as my muscles warm up in the morning sun. Over one
hundred miles ahead, a rocky peak glimmers on the horizon.
The view defines expanse in a big west Texas sky. I come to a stop
miles from civilization. Cows stare at me, wondering about my
sanity. A touch of wind lifts my hair off my sweaty neck. I raise my

hands with open palms high above my head to touch the stillness. My breathing makes the only sound. The ache of delight is almost unbearable. Joni

Joyful, Joyful, We Adore Thee
Hymn by Henry van Dyke

Joyful, joyful, we adore Thee,
God of glory, Lord of love;
Hearts unfold like flowers before Thee,
Opening to the sun above.
Melt the clouds of sin and sadness;
Drive the dark of doubt away;
Giver of immortal gladness,
Fill us with the light of day!
All Thy works with joy surround Thee,
Earth and heaven reflect Thy rays,
Stars and angels sing around Thee,
Center of unbroken praise.
Field and forest, vale and mountain,
Flowering meadow, flashing sea,
Singing bird and flowing fountain,
Call us to rejoice in Thee.

 Where and how have you engaged God's creation in the past month? The past year? Did you see God there?

The sacred does not insist on its sacredness. It is there to be experienced—or not. It is essentially shy. It is patient, not demanding. We can seek it out, reverence it, turn our lives toward it, or we can walk right past it, preoccupied with our own affairs. Daniel Taylor

The camera always goes on vacation with us. A visit to our home reveals ample photographic artifacts of Pyne family adventures. Smiling faces intersperse sunsets, waterfalls and flowers. All of us love a good vista. Our youngest son made an insightful comment recently. We were driving around town, running errands or something equally unexciting. A sunset loomed in front of the windshield. "If we were on vacation, you would stop and take a picture of that," Ben astutely remarked. My preoccupation with the mundane had blunted my appreciation of God's artistic display. I heard the Spirit call to me through Ben's words. Delight looms as close as our windshield, definitely worth the picture anytime. **Bob**

The Peace of Wild Things
by Wendell Berry

When despair for the world grows in me
and I wake in the night at the least sound
in fear of what my life and my children's lives may be,
I go and lie down where the wood drake
rests in his beauty on the water, and the great heron feeds.
I come into the peace of wild things
who do not tax their lives with forethought
of grief. I come into the presence of still water.
And I feel above me the day-blind stars
waiting with their light. For a time
I rest in the grace of the world, and am free.

My hometown church spawned several Sword Drill champions. You sheathed your Bible under your left arm. The Quizmaster (no, I did not make that name up) then said, "Draw your swords!" and you brought the Bible almost to eye-level with arms outstretched. Either hand could be on top of the Bible, but no fingers were allowed to touch the pages. Thumbs were often culprits. With arms trembling from anxiety, you waited for "Charge!" when you dove into your Bible to beat everyone else in locating the announced passage. Competition proved fierce and sometimes vicious. The state competition required brand-new Bibles for the drill. What a sensuous treat to bury your nose in the crisp inked pages. **Joni**

Does the Word of God lead you to see and delight in the person of God? How has the Word functioned in your practice of life with God? Have you moved beyond Sword Drill?

Re-text us
by Walter Brueggemann

We confess you to be text-maker,
        text-giver,
        text-worker,
   and we find ourselves addressed
      by your making, giving, working,
So now we bid you, re-text us by your spirit.
      Re-text us away from our shallow loves,
         into your overwhelming gracefulness.
      Re-text us away from our thin angers,
         into your truth-telling freedom.
      Re-text us away from our lean hopes,
         into your tidal promises.
Give us attentive ears,
      responsive hearts,
      receiving hands;
         Re-text us to be your liberated partners
           in joy and obedience,
           in risk and gratitude.
Re-text us by your word become wind. Amen.

• • • • •

Psalm 139 became my scriptural home during college. My daily devotional time regularly ended there. I would meditate on the expansive description of God's mysterious, all-knowing presence. The final two verses asked God to search me, to reveal any wicked ways and to lead me in the "way everlasting." I camped on these verses (often literally, as I fell asleep on my Bible at night). I wrote out my areas of struggle and need for improvement. My notebook filled with resolutions covering perceived failures and daily recommitments to change. But I could not see my own self-absorption. The psalmist would have grieved at my narrow use of the Word. What started with gazing upon the person of God ended with my own box-building. **Bob**

Psalm 95

For the L ORD is a great God,
And a great King above all gods,
In whose hand are the depths of the earth;
The peaks of the mountains are His also.
The sea is His, for it was He who made it;
And His hands formed the dry land.
Come, let us worship and bow down;
Let us kneel before the L ORD our Maker.
For He is our God,
And we are the people of His pasture,
and the sheep of His hand.

Are you open to the mystery of the Word of God? Do you separate the Word of God from the person of God in order to control its effect? Do you allow the Spirit room to bring you delight through the Word?

From Psalm 145 …

The LORD is trustworthy in all he promises
and faithful in all he does.
The LORD upholds all who fall
and lifts up all who are bowed down.
The eyes of all look to you,
and you give them their food at the proper time.
You open your hand
and satisfy the desires of every living thing.
The LORD is righteous in all his ways
and faithful in all he does.
The LORD is near to all who call on him,
to all who call on him in truth.
He fulfills the desires of those who fear him;
he hears their cry and saves them….
My mouth will speak in praise of the LORD.
Let every creature praise his holy name
for ever and ever.

●　　●　　●　　●　　●

A stack of three Bibles sits on my work desk—different English translations of the same Word. Over a hundred more exist for those interested in exploring them. I move between translations as I write. Many theologians would not join me in that approach, claiming the accuracy of one translation over others. Arguments ensue over the deft handling of letters and sentences. When Joni and I taught in Rwanda, our words and the Word were translated into Kinyarwanda, of which we knew not one single syllable. The translator quickly became our new best friend. We had no idea how what we said translated into what the pastors heard. The Spirit wrested the Word of God out of our hands, taking it to the hearts of the people in their own language. It was liberating, to be honest, to trust God with the mystery of the Word. As well it should be. **Bob**

1129
by Emily Dickinson

Tell all the Truth but tell it slant—
Success in Circuit lies
Too bright for our infirm Delight
The Truth's superb surprise
As Lightning to the Children eased
With explanation kind
The Truth must dazzle gradually
Or every man be blind—

•   •   •   •   •

Writing this book has tied me to the computer for months. Literally unending days of words come at me. The letters mock me as they dance around the page late at night. To be honest, some days I swear off reading or writing for the rest of my life. To counteract this unfortunate attitude, I employ my favorite communal discipline: eating chocolate with teenage daughters. The girls tumble through the front door after school, brim full of words for me. I can be quiet. I practice listening well. The chocolate encourages conversation. The tall daughter, Kate, drapes her lounge-y, lank-y self all over me, vacillating between sophistication and eating pudding with her index finger. God graces me with delight in all that it is to be young. What a nice respite after all those words. **Joni**

 Do you honor humanity as created to bear God's image? What of humanity turns your gaze toward God? Do you look for God's face in the people around you? Are you moved to delight?

•   •   •   •   •

They decided to get the mother from the nursing home at the last minute. Surely she wanted to be at her son's funeral. Here came the little walnut of a woman, almost bouncing out of her wheelchair as her grandson pushed her up and over the cemetery plots. Everyone stood, hushed, as the young man lifted the mother to look into the casket. "Yep. That's him alright!" she pronounced loudly, as if an imposter had been suspected. At that very moment, bees swarmed out of the casket flowers and began dive-bombing those of us standing nearby. Some people thought our bodies were racked with sobs as the service progressed. Little did they know. **Joni**

Old Folks Laugh
by Maya Angelou

They have spent their
content of simpering,
holding their lips this
and that way, winding
the lines between
their brows. Old folks
allow their bellies to jiggle like slow
tamborines.
The hollers
rise up and spill
over any way they want.
When old folks laugh, they free the world.
They turn slowly, slyly knowing
the best and the worst
of remembering.
Saliva glistens in
the corners of their mouths,
their heads wobble
on brittle necks, but
their laps
are filled with memories.
When old folks laugh, they consider the promise
of dear painless death, and generously
forgive life for happening
to them.

The old farmer had a spare, perfunctory funeral. No fanfare or pomp and circumstance—just to the old man's liking. He was headed home to heaven. We dawdled as the last ones to leave the cemetery. As we turned to get in our car, here came the farmer in his last hurrah. A big green tractor was pulling his casket on wheels down the lane to the graveside. The tractor chugged by the car, followed by the tottering casket, its wheels clattering down the black-dirt road. We waved. The perfect send-off. **Joni**

I asked the men at a retreat to describe how they saw God's glory displayed in humanity. Until that hour, the time in Kansas had been a little frosty. Not only did the winter wind whip around the church building, but also the men of the plains kept their thoughts close to their chests, zipped up under shearling vests. Tears began to roll down one man's face. There was this two-year-old boy, you see, a child born to his unmarried daughter—his own grandson made in the image of God. All kinds of explanations lay on the table, but the bottom line saw this man living in a hard place of judgment and rejection. The warm wind of the Spirit began to move, thawing a grandfather's heart. **Bob**

We call Monte the artist "our little brother." He takes a discarded photograph and extracts one interesting, tiny segment as the foundation for his art. Nice touch in using that which has been discarded to produce beauty. Monte looked over my shoulder as I edited some sunrise pictures from a recent trip. I predictably turned the digital images right side up. Monte abruptly said "Stop!" For him, the sunrises looked perfect sideways. Art right side up. Monte approaches life chest open, laying aside presumptions about reality and broadening the horizon of sight. I like to engage the practice of life with God the same way. It keeps things lively. **Joni**

Where do you find delight in aesthetic beauty? Can you see the Creator God's reflection in human creativity? What role does art, music, literature, dance—any venue of humanity's creative expression—play in your enjoyment of God?

•   •   •   •   ●

Whenever I go to Madrid, my feet invariably find their way to El Museo de Prado. Each time I go to the same room on the second floor of this lavish museum. Before me hangs El Greco's luminous series on Christ. Huge paintings tower to the top of the two-story ceilings: the Nativity, the Crucifixion, the Ascension, the Trinity. The paint's aged patina glows in the soft light. The artist's imagination explodes in the narrative detail of each treasure. I throw my head back and close my eyes as tears run down my cheeks and chills down my spine. Transcendent beauty never fails to move me. That room and those paintings are a gift of joy from the Spirit of God: El Greco flaying my heart open with the stroke of his hand. Joni

I can't stand the holy at full strength. I need it mediated—through a poem, through a biography, through a story—through an island. I go to Iona and Lindisfarne and Skellig Michael to get a tangible taste of an intangible and fearful reality. But I want only a taste. Like the Israelites at Sinai, I want God to speak to Moses, not me. Daniel Taylor

•   •   •   •   ●

Aunt Frankie brings her famous green chili cheese grits to every funeral dinner. Everyone prays they get a spoonful. What better way to thumb your nose at death than to partake in such heart-stopping fare? The cackling cooks arrive en masse at the family's home. Masking-tape labels identify their cake pans, and rooster potholders cover hot handles. These women come as life-givers standing in the doorway of grief. Sustenance is their gift, cheese grits their art. **Joni**

●   ●   ●   ●   ●

The brazen boldness of youth inspires me. Our teenage son almost missed his orchestra concert last night. He hurriedly shed the baseball uniform for the tuxedo. "I forgot my music," Danny said on the way to the auditorium. Unfortunately, so did the other bass players. All four of them lined up behind empty music stands as the concert began. A less-confident soul might have been stymied by this turn of events. Danny picked up his bow, capitalized on the notes he knew and improvised around the general melody—loudly and with gusto—smiling, of course. I think about Danny's response and how it applies to the discipline of delight. Find a note and jump into the process. Make some music. Enthusiasm counts. **Bob**

Sometimes in their chanting monks will land upon a note and sing it in florid fashion, one syllable of text for fifty notes of chant. *Melisma,* they call it.... Living a *melismatic* life in imitation of plainchant, we may stop on an experience, a place, a person, or a memory and rhapsodize in imagination.... Living one point after another is one form of experience, and it can be emphatically productive. But stopping for *melisma* gives the soul its reason for being. Thomas Moore

●   ●   ●   ●   ●

My wife, Julie, and I took in the twilight beauty alongside a high mountain lake. On the pebbled beach, a rock cairn stood like a precarious sentry. Very quirky and whimsical. Stones and sticks balanced miraculously on the sand. The creative impulse of the human artist brought smiles to our faces. The stars shone brightly that night, their reflections sparkling across the water. They started at the sky's apex and splashed playfully all the way down to the horizon. The divine Creator enveloped the creature's handiwork. **Bob**

To delight in the good of all the universe, but not to delight in God, is like being glad that a candle is lit, but being indifferent to the rising sun. John Piper

*   *   *   *   ●

My family has tired of my new mantra: "goat cheese." For years I did not like goat cheese. At the height of its popularity in chic restaurants, I campaigned against its pungent presence. But a person can easily become stodgy, brittle and inelastic. After reconsideration, I am now one of goat cheese's biggest fans. Do not ask me how it happened. Things change. Something about exploring new horizons as well as revisiting old ones. I travel on an adventure by myself each year—kayaking or climbing or anything that scares me to death. Life seems more acute balancing on top of a granite spire. God meets me out there on joy's frontier. Have you tried anything new lately? Try goat cheese as a safe place to start. **Joni**

We hope you enjoyed the slices of delight you found in these pages. We pray they stimulate your appetite for more. Keep your eyes open. Look for clues. Practice being fully human as you celebrate God's glory. The Holy Spirit brings us into a reality beyond ourselves. Joy awaits us there.

The human connection runs throughout this chapter. You see human beings encountering their Creator and each other. The next chapter, "Rope," acknowledges our creation as communal beings called to fellowship together. Loving well becomes a distinctive mark in our practice of life with God.

My mouth will speak
in praise of the LORD.
Let every creature praise
his holy name for ever and ever.

Psalm 145

chapter seven

RO

OPE

A mausoleum in Delhi, India, honors Mahatma Gandhi as the hero of Indian independence. The building front prominently displays a quotation from Gandhi: TRUTH IS GOD. As you stop to ponder the words for a moment, something seems right and yet odd. Your head cocks to the side, trying to get a different perspective.

As followers of Christ—the Way, the Truth, and the Life—we reverse the words: God is truth. The entire meaning changes with the reordering. If the sign is right, humans define truth. You define it, we define it, the next person on the street defines it. Essentially, your truth becomes your god—so convenient for box building! If the Bible is right, then God defines truth. Our experience of truth ever expands as our knowledge of God increases.

As with truth, we often make a mistake in defining love. Ads urge you to love your car or your wristwatch. Books warn you about loving too much. Seminars teach you the languages of love. There could be a sign on the front of our buildings: LOVE IS GOD. When we define love apart from God, our definition is convoluted and skewed at best, perverted at worst. We mistake money, fame, power, lust, need, jealousy and other placebos for love. Such misperceptions are bankrupt and devoid of redemptive power. Life turns upside down.

The person of God defines the truth of love: God is love. God is love in its pure form—unadulterated, untainted, boundless.

In "Shift," we explore the Holy Spirit's transformation of our love. Fulfilling our created purpose, we come to reflect the glorious perfections of God for God's own sake. We begin to love *what* God loves and *how* God loves. In our practice of life with God, we obey the foremost commandments of Christ: loving God with all our being and loving the community of humanity. We move from being drains to fountains as the Spirit shifts our gaze from the self outward in love, resulting in an ever-increasing enjoyment of God.

In this chapter, we first look at the character of perfect love in the person of God. As the Holy Spirit works in us to love *what* God loves, the imperative of community surfaces. We then move to the call to love others well, aligning our affection with *how* God loves.

We use words such as "love" and "community" often in this book. The words may be clichés to many people, like pictures of a pretty sunset or a cute baby. Yeah, yeah. Love, love. Community, community. Do unto others, do unto others. Got it, got it. Peace, love, dove, man. Maybe your experience makes you cynical about these topics. Stay with us. The chapter twists and turns in surprising ways.

source of love

Within the triad of faith, hope and love, scripture elevates love as first above the others. The pronouncement "God is love" assigns the immensity and limitlessness of God to the matter of love. An old hymn beautifully wraps human language around the idea:

The love of God is greater far
Than tongue or pen can ever tell.
It goes beyond the highest star
And reaches to the lowest hell.
The guilty pair, bowed down with care,
God gave His Son to win.

His erring child He reconciled
And pardoned from his sin.
Could we with ink the ocean fill,
And were the skies of parchment made,
Were every stalk on earth a quill,

And every man a scribe by trade,
To write the love of God above
Would drain the ocean dry.
Nor could the scroll contain the whole,
Though stretched from sky to sky.

O love of God, how rich and pure!
How measureless and strong!
It shall forevermore endure:
The saints' and angels' song.

• • • • • stop a moment

Reread the words of the hymn. If you happen to know the tune, hum along as you read. Organize a sing-along if you have it in you. Beyond the highest star and reaching to the lowest hell. An ocean filled with ink and a parchment stretched across the sky. God reached down to reconcile an erring child with love.

Can you wrap your thoughts around the immensity and intimacy of that picture? What would it be like to live in the center of that love and to believe in its power? Do you make God's love small and manageable like biting off a tiny corner of taffy so it does not stick in your teeth?

• • • • •

Paul wrote his letter to the Ephesians while in a Roman prison. Yet he used expansive language similar to the hymn in describing the love of Christ:

> I pray that, according to the riches of his glory, he may grant that you may be strengthened in your inner being with power through his Spirit, and that Christ may dwell in your hearts through faith, as you are being rooted and grounded in love. I pray that you may have the power to

comprehend, with all the saints, what is the breadth and length and height and depth, and to know the love of Christ that surpasses knowledge, so that you may be filled with all the fullness of God.

Imagine a waterfall of love plunging down on you. The water washes over you and rushes around you. Your arms open wide and your face lifts to feel the water's power. But where does all that water go? Do you think of it pooling endlessly at your feet or rising until your nose barely pokes out for air? When you think of God's love, do you see yourself as a passive receptacle, waiting for the water to fill you up? The water must flow or it will stagnate. God's love is on the move.

Like a river that never runs dry, Christ flings unbounded, gracious love. Taking that love and turning inward, shining up our medals and shoring up our boxes, stifles love's power. Transformation happens when we give God's love away.

law of love

Remember the scribe who quizzed Jesus on the preeminent commandment? Jesus responded with the law of love: Love God with all your being and love your neighbor as you love yourself. The medieval theologian Thomas Aquinas aptly observed we ought to love others "because they are nigh to us, both as to the natural image of God, and as to the capacity for glory." We love the reflection of God's glory in our neighbor.

Jesus' response to the scribe points to the communal nature of life with God. The triune God exists in eternal fellowship. From Genesis forward, we see God act in relationship. Our inward turn of sin shuns God's overture of love. The gospel of Christ brings a reconciled relationship between God and humanity, inviting us back into the triune communion. Redemption occurs in both the vertical relationship with God and the horizontal relationship with others.

You cannot opt out of community. You commune well or poorly, but you do commune in the very act of being human.

You cannot opt out of community

A revelation of love illuminated this point for author Donald Miller: "I was being asked to walk away from the lies I believed about the world being about me. I had been communicating unlove to my housemates because I thought they were not cooperating with the meaning of life, that meaning being my desire and will and choice and comfort."

The Spirit's work in transforming our affection shifts our focus. We move from isolation to community, from using others to seeking their greatest good, from the self-centered need for control to freedom for others to breathe, from glaring at that ex-girlfriend across the church aisle to offering your hand during the passing of peace.

> This is my commandment, that you love one another as I have loved you. No one has greater love than this, to lay down one's life for one's friends. You are my friends if you do what I command you. John 15

The Spirit uses fellow humans as a means of transformation and also makes that transformation visible through fellow humans. Our friend and theologian LeRon Shults aptly observed, "All of our lives are spent longing for a face that will grant us peaceful loving attention, a face that will secure us and call us into a hopeful future. In Christ, we find that face; by the Spirit, we become that face for one another."

> Owe no one anything, except to love one another; for the one who loves another has fulfilled the law.

The commandments, "You shall not commit adultery; You shall not murder; You shall not steal; You shall not covet"; and any other commandment, are summed up in this word, "Love your neighbor as yourself." Love does no wrong to a neighbor; therefore, love is the fulfilling of the law. Romans 13

The Bible pushes hard against the cultural definitions of "neighbor" in both ancient and modern times. The story of the Good Samaritan in Luke 10 tells of a man beaten by robbers and left for dead. His countrymen pass by without stopping, ignoring the man's need. A Samaritan, considered an enemy in the ethnic wars of the day, tends to the man's wounds and pays for his care. Christ expanded the traditional concept of neighbor exponentially with this parable.

Along these lines, Karl Barth introduced the concepts of "near neighbor" and "far neighbor." From the first human relationship between husband and wife, then including children, then outward to friends and acquaintances, followed by humanity at large, the commandment to love throws a wide net over the whole. Barth described a call to move from "the narrower sphere to a wider," allowing the concept of one's own people to be fluid:

The movement leads us relentlessly, however, from the narrower sphere to a wider, from our own people to other human peoples. . . . And the command of God wills that a man should really move out from his beginning and therefore seek a wider field. He will have to overcome a certain reluctance to do so. He will always be accompanied by some measure of homesickness . . . the concepts of home, motherland and people, while they must retain their original sense, will prove capable of extension.

We mentioned a trip to Rwanda previously. We went with Celestin, a former student of mine and a Rwandan pastor. Julie and I met Celestin and his family during his time in seminary. Celestin repeatedly encouraged me to visit his country, and our schedules finally coincided this past summer.

Knowing Celestin and Bernadette and their children brought one level of friendship. Meeting the people of Rwanda and seeing Celestin in his native environment yielded a wholly different level of friendship. I saw the loving greetings of a congregation for their pastor: a kiss on each cheek followed by an embracing handshake.

I met Celestin's closest colleagues and heard their dreams for ministry. I stayed with Celestin, ate with him, prayed with him and laughed with him. Joni and I taught Rwandan pastors for a week, soaking in their easy smiles and soulful brown eyes. I heard their transcendent, harmonic singing as my wake-up call early each morning.

Celestin was the bridge to my far neighbors, a distant people to whom I am inextricably tied in my humanity. I miss their faces and the intriguing sound of their language. I miss seeing Celestin in their midst. I am richer for having gone to Rwanda, but I continue to pay a price for the trip. I will never get used to the buzz of a strident alarm clock after hearing a spontaneous, angelic choir celebrate the sunrise.

● ● ● ● ●

The inclination to dwell with those who you know, who look like you and who agree with you runs strong. It takes courage and boldness to move beyond that border. Within the church, we often find the narrowest definition of neighbor. One of our church fellows recently said, "We are not supposed to love people until they come to Christ." Oh, really? How are they supposed to come to Christ unless they see God's love in us?

The Spirit uses other people as agents of change in our lives. Moving outward from home to the near and distant neighbors introduces new realities that expand our horizons.

In this is love, not that we loved God but that he loved us and sent his Son to be the atoning sacrifice for our sins. Beloved, since God loved us so much, we also ought to love one another. No one has ever seen God; if we love one another, God lives in us, and his love is perfected in us. 1 John 4

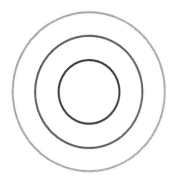

• • • • • stop a moment

Complete this diagram of your sphere of community. Starting inside the smallest circle, jot a sample of names representing your closest community. Your immediate family would typically be here along, perhaps, with others. In the next circle moving outward, jot a sample of names to represent your near neighbors, your friends and colleagues that complete your primary community. In the outermost circle, jot names of people or groups who are your far neighbors. These are the people on the farthest horizon of community for you. They push your boundaries. These people may or may not be geographically distant from you.

One last item: In the free space outside the largest circle, put the names of any person or group you might consider your enemy or for any reason you find yourself unable to love. These may be individuals or ethnic groups or political groups or maybe people in places far beyond your comfort zone. Perhaps it is the gay couple that lives next door to you. Or your brother-in-law. Use initials if you feel the need to be discrete here.

Look at the completed diagram. Do you seek to move from the narrower sphere to the wider? Do your relationships demonstrate openness to extension? Where do your prejudices lie? Do you believe the Spirit can truly transform the affection of your heart in the community you claim? Can you envision your circles expanding to encompass the last names you wrote?

In Matthew 5, Christ says, "You have heard that it was said, 'You shall love your neighbor and hate your enemy.' But I say to you, Love your enemies and pray for those who persecute you." Loving people who love you surprises no one. Love shines distinctively as it moves beyond the expected.

Is a church fellowship of any kind on your diagram? Perhaps in the smallest circle, representing a close, familial relationship with a local community of believers in Christ? If you are like Sam, then a church fellowship might be, at best, in the outer circle or even beyond the boundaries. Maybe there is nothing about church anywhere in the picture.

We believe the fellowship of believers should be a driving force for an outward gaze and an expansion of your world. Are you connected to a church community that pushes you beyond your comfort zone? Or is it a safe place to hide from the Really Real?

•   •   •   •   •

People act as mirrors to help us align reality with our often misinformed perceptions. They affirm change in our lives, encouraging us in the transformation process. And community constantly calls us to abandon self-absorption. It is a powerful antidote to navel-gazing. Frederick Buechner described this work of God in one of his signature lengthy sentences:

What is both Good and New about the Good News is the mad insistence that Jesus lives on among us not just as another haunting memory but as the outlandish, holy, and invisible power of God working not just through the sacraments but in countless hidden ways to make even slobs like us loving and whole beyond anything we could conceivably pull off ourselves.

way of love

Technical rock climbing requires specialized skill and specific gear. A harness attaches each person to the climbing rope. You fit the harness around your waist and both legs, using special loops to secure the webbing around the buckles. The rope attaches to the harness using specific knots that, when tied correctly, are failsafe. The rope typically extends from one harness to at least one other. In many climbing parties, several people share the same rope.

Progress up and down the climbing route requires that all the people on the rope move in tandem. A climber learns particular phrases to aid communication within the group. "Belay." "Belay on." "Climbing." "Climb on." The hardest one to remember is "Falling!" Most people just scream.

Climbing together feels like a delicate dance: taking rope and giving rope, securing rope and releasing rope. New climbers might step on the rope or move too fast or hang on the rope instead of the rock. Climbing with anyone requires courtesy, communication and cooperation.

Being roped together is a helpful metaphor for the way of love. Pulitzer Prize-winning columnist, Leonard Pitts, Jr., put it well: "To love somebody is to make yourself hostage to the fortunes of others. It is to give a hundred people veto power over your happiness." Individualism can attempt to exclude the other, denying the connection. Even a distorted idea of tolerance can inappropriately reject otherness, causing us to revolve in a world that embraces nothing.

• • • • • a story from Joni

We hiked up the glacier with our crampons and ice axes. While I looked, in my humble opinion, quite the seasoned adventurer on the outside, I wondered why on earth I had willingly paid money for this. Had I lost my mind?

Rocco, the quintessential guide, came to a stop as we faced a tall rock spire. He roped us together, we put on our climbing shoes, and Rocco prepared to swing around the corner of a boulder and onto the face of the rock. He looked over his shoulder and asked, "How do you feel about exposure?" Was there some expectation of climbing less than clothed? What did he mean? I answered naively, "Oh, fine."

As I followed Rocco around the corner, I unexpectedly encountered the face of a cliff with a sheer drop of 200 feet below me—ending in a deep crevasse—and a climb of 100 feet above me. Plastering myself against the cold, slick face, I clung to the rock. The guide snapped a picture of me from above. I looked terrified and ecstatic at the same time.

The question "How do you feel about exposure?" rings true for life tied to other people. We cling together on this adventure with 200 feet below us and 100 feet above. I am exposed in the vulnerability of my relationship with you. My incurvature is futile self-protection to lessen your impact on my life. Loving as God loves means to turn outward, rope up with gusto, swing around the corner and celebrate the climb. • • • • •

We cannot live the law of love apart from community. Wesleyan scholar Theodore Runyon wrote, "To turn Christianity into a solitary religion is to destroy it, for it can no longer function as it was designed to function, to communicate renewing grace to others." Closing ourselves up in a monk's cell, with a slit in the door for the nightly bowl of gruel, does not teach obedience to love what and how God loves. Church congregations exist in recognition of our communal calling. Their success or failure depends on their openness to the movement of the Holy Spirit, who aligns the hearts of the people with the heart of God.

> I appeal to you therefore, brothers and sisters, by the mercies of God, to present your bodies as a living sacrifice, holy and acceptable to God, which is your spiritual worship. Do not be conformed to this world, but be transformed by the renewing of your minds, so that you may discern what is the will of God—what is good and acceptable and perfect.

You hear those first two verses of Romans 12 quoted frequently in church circles as a call to transformation. We often take a wrong turn at this juncture by assuming this call encompasses the individual alone. These verses must be read in the context of the command to love. The good and acceptable and perfect will of God is to love God and others well. The balance of the chapter in Romans refers, in fact, to the fellowship of human beings. Love without hypocrisy. Rejoice and weep with others. To the extent it depends on you, be at peace with all people.

• • • • • a story from Bob

I approached my doctoral studies very seriously. Time could not be squandered. I remember one particular day in the library, doing research for my dissertation. A friend I had not seen in a very long time walked through the entry of the building. Her face lit up as she came toward me, obviously expecting a chat to catch up on life. I was busy—very busy. I gave a cursory smile, said "Hey, how are you?" and kept walking. Minimal contact meant I could not be captured for time-consuming chatting. I hate to think what it felt like for my friend to stare at my back.

I still regret that day almost twenty years later. As if five minutes, ten minutes or an hour would have changed the course of my dissertation. My regret stems from the conscious choice I made against loving well. What I gained was nothing compared to what I lost. The commandment to love plays out in just such discrete moments of our days. We make choices to engage the other or to look away. Neither convenience nor efficiency fit the vocabulary of communing well.

•　　•　　•　　•　　•

Some people use the "sin lists" or "vice lists" of Ephesians 4 and Galatians 5 as a treasury of box-building materials. Read through these passages. The lists are all relational in nature. Grieving the Spirit comes from loving poorly. We spend time boxing ourselves in with rules of what we will not do, while ignoring the command to love. "Be kind to one another, tenderhearted, forgiving one another. Live in love, as Christ loved us and gave himself up for us."

Loving well recognizes the effect one human life has upon another. Barth wrote, "I am as Thou art." Your well-being organically connects to the well-being of your neighbor. As Buechner states:

> Your life and my life flow into each other as wave flows into wave, and unless there is peace and joy and freedom for you, there can be no real peace and joy and freedom for me.

•　　•　　•　　•　　• **a story from Joni**

Hannah (Tim's and my eldest daughter) and I went on a mountaineering trip with a good friend, Sara. Hannah climbs like a ballet dancer on the rock. A beautiful sight to watch.

She certainly did not think waking up at 3:45 A.M. to summit a mountain was an appropriate summer activity, but she placated me and went along with a smile. OK, mostly a smile. We captured the summit on a clear, sunny day. The expansive, 360-degree view at the top made the effort worthwhile. Granola bars provided fuel for the trip back to camp.

The descent proved more precarious than anticipated. I led, with Hannah roped between Sara and me. We had to traverse a particularly tricky section without being able to see where to place our feet. I looked back and talked Hannah through the moves from my vantage point. At one juncture, she exclaimed, "Mom, I am going to die!" Yes, this was our summer vacation. What fun! I answered, "Hannah, you will have to wait to die until after you get Sara across that rock." She magnanimously laid aside her own fear as she focused on helping Sara climb down.

My reaction has been the source of much laughter this side of that climb. Sorry, but you will have to postpone death. Right now someone needs you in order to get off this mountain. We are roped together. Every move I make—and do not make—affects the whole.

• • • • •

Life intertwined with others
will be messy and inelegant.

Community is complicated. We lurch along the rope. One of us sticks her crampons into a snow bank and takes the entire group down as she flails about. One makes a huge move over a boulder and pulls the others off the rock. One never remembers how to tie his knots correctly or keep the rope coiled. We love well some days and poorly others. Our transformation by the Spirit takes an eternity. Forget about shortcuts.

We believe success in loving well begins with showing up. Skin on skin. Looking another in the eye. Embrace the concept of lollygagging—being together without a three-point agenda. It represents a high art form that takes a lifetime of practice. Choose an afternoon chat over accomplishing ten errands in under an hour.

lollygagging represents a high art form

Loving well means pushing against the mantra of "Speed is God. Time is the devil." Turn off your multiple phones, the television, your computer and all the other technological wonders of connectivity. Show up in the flesh.

Eat lunch with your child at school. Go see your mother on her birthday. Stop by your colleague's office in lieu of sending a message. Read books aloud with your best friend. Go to a funeral and cry with the family. Hand-deliver that baby gift instead of putting it in the mail. Take food along as you go. Live slowly and shock everyone. Exchange efficiency for the richness and dimension and color of loving community. The Spirit moves among real people in real relationships spending real time together.

• • • • • a story from Bob

The news stunned our boys' baseball team: a favorite player killed by his own father, who then committed suicide. The father had been at a game four days before, yelling and chatting along with all the parents. Who had any idea what was to come?

A crowd gathered at the baseball field for an informal service of remembrance. As the candles burned low, everyone placed the short stubs of wax in the dirt behind home plate. The team formed a tight circle to watch the last flame flicker out. Comrades in sadness, they wandered en masse from home plate, to center field, to the dugout—not wanting to leave. Being together meant they were accounted for and alive. They took comfort in the evidence of simply being present.

• • • • •

It is the task of those who believe and those who love
to extend the great divine Yes to life,
which we find in Christ and in the holy Spirit of life,
arouse pleasure in living, and preserve the memory
not only of suffering but also of resurrection.

Jürgen Moltmann

Anchored in the faithfulness of God, we can fling love fearlessly
and with abandon upon our neighbors. "How do you feel about
exposure?" "Bring it on!" we yell back.

Neither death, nor life, nor angels, nor rulers, nor things
present, nor things to come, nor powers, nor height, nor
depth, nor anything else in all creation, will be able to
separate us from the love of God in Christ Jesus our
Lord. Romans 8

What would it be like for the people in your life to hear you
say those words about your love for them? Do you love uncon-
ditionally, without using love as a negotiating tool to manipu-
late others for your purposes? Loving others as God loves them
will burn you up as the Holy Spirit calls you over and over to
die to self.

The next chapters, "Space," "Gift" and "Fool," examine the
distinctive marks of love in grace, forgiveness and sacrifice.
In these dimensions, *how* we love reflects God's glory and
leads us toward being fully human. We follow Christ into a
life of relationship, equipped by the Spirit to love God and
others well.

Forget about reading more words for the moment. Put this
book down. Go show up somewhere for someone. Be really
real in flesh and blood. Practice lollygagging. Watch for joy.

Teach us to care, teach us to use all these occasions of need that are the agenda of our work as access to God, as access to neighbor.
Teach us to care by teaching us to pray, to pray so that human need becomes the occasion for entering into and embracing the presence and action of God in this life. Teach us to care by teaching us to pray so that those with whom we work are not less human through our caring but become more human. Teach us to care so that we do not become collaborators in self-centeredness, but rather companions in God-exploration. Teach us to use each act of caring as an act of praying so that this person in the act of being cared for experiences dignity instead of condescension, realizes the glory of being in on the salvation, and blessing, and healing of God, and is not driven further into neurosis and the wasteland of self.

Eugene Peterson

LifeSpace

chapter eight

SPA

ACE

glory-reflecting

fracture-healing   hope-renewing

G
R
love-flinging   A   space-creating
C
E

self-forgetting   image-honoring

life-giving

celebration

Writing about grace in a dignified, somber fashion feels weird. There should be a raucous celebration of dancing in the streets, with shouting and cavorting. Our mouths should gape at the beauty of grace and our minds contort over the mystery of grace.

Grace holds the space for you to be while you are becoming. It creates the expanse to breathe so you do not die. These pages could not contain grace even with flawless crafting of each letter and comma. It leaps off the paper and into your life.

If you tear out all the songs in a hymnal that mention grace, you would have only a few sheets left between the covers. You may say grace for the food at the dinner table. Perhaps your kids fight over who has to or gets to say it. Did you notice Joni's name on the cover of this book? She is a Grace in a long line of Graces. Grace seems to be common in our lives, so why the call to celebration?

Through grace, we have the privilege to commune with and delight in God forever. In unequivocal freedom, God extends grace in the act of giving the gift of redemption through Jesus Christ the Son. Kindness rains down upon us. The Holy Spirit's breath expands our lungs. By God's favor, not by our human right, we truly live.

God bestows the grace of undeserved, unearned, unmerited favor on humanity.

We join God in the act of giving as we, in turn, extend the gift of favor to the people in our lives. The idea of loving well, emphasized in "Rope," pivots on this extension of grace. We become life-givers as we create space for people to practice life with God, pilgrims together. Give your spouse space to like goat cheese or bungee-jumping. Give your son space to be in that garage band. Give your pastor space to try a new hairstyle. How about giving yourself a pass to do one new thing this week or *not* do one old thing? Transformation happens in these spaces of grace.

Philip Yancey wrote, "Grace teaches us that God loves because of who God is, not because of who we are." How hard we strive against those words. Masking tape and straight-lined boxes feed our pride as we work to earn God's love. It feels disappointing without the spotlight on us. Or maybe we have voiced complete disinterest, but the Spirit refuses to let us alone. We run the other way, trying to shake God off.

God acts freely out of unfettered love toward us, with no external requirement or inner necessity. Perplexed at this motive, we are often at a loss to receive grace, well, graciously. Surely there is something we should be *doing* or *not* doing.

Gracious is the LORD, and righteous; our God is merciful. The LORD protects the simple; when I was brought low, he saved me. Return, O my soul, to your rest, for the LORD has dealt bountifully with you. For you have delivered my soul from death, my eyes from tears, my feet from stumbling. I walk before the LORD in the land of the living. Psalm 116

• • • • • a story from Joni

During my childhood, revival preachers would come through town for a week's crusade at least once a year. They usually came in one of two flavors: either deadly serious with a bit of a mortician's demeanor or colorfully flamboyant with bouffant hair. The former scared me. The latter were my favorites. Our family went to the revival nightly without fail. No excuses. Sunday attire mandatory. The preachers were my rock stars. I had my bulletin autographed whenever I could.

Each evening would end with an invitation to accept the gospel of Christ. One evangelist would lean precariously over the podium. A bony finger pointed, it seemed, right at me. In an otherworldly voice, the questions would rain down: "If you were to die tonight, do you know beyond a shadow of a doubt that you will go to heaven? If you were to die tonight, do you know beyond a shadow of a doubt that you will not burn in the fires of hell?"

The "beyond a shadow of a doubt" part always tripped me up. I professed a saving faith in Christ, but there were so many sins since the last evangelist had been to town. Could grace really be that big? Surely I had not tried hard enough.

Down the aisle I would fly toward the front. Sobbing, I would rededicate my life to the glory of God. One more time. It came to the point where someone in my family would throw an arm in front of me the minute the evangelist's finger appeared.

It took a long time for me to grasp the immensity of God's grace. Honestly, it still eludes me.

• • • • •

He destined us for adoption as his children through Jesus Christ, according to the good pleasure of his will, to the praise of his glorious grace that he freely bestowed on us in the Beloved. In him we have redemption through his blood, the forgiveness of our trespasses, according to the riches of his grace that he lavished on us. Ephesians 1

Michael Malone, a friend and one of our favorite Southern authors, wrote a novel titled *Handling Sin*. Think *Don Quixote* of the South. Raleigh Hayes, the lead character, had his life in perfect balance: Everything and everyone was under control. An insurance salesman, he staked his life on the two most important values: safety and security.

On a bizarre road trip to New Orleans in search of his errant father—last seen checking out of a hospital and heading out of town with a young woman in a Cadillac convertible—Raleigh's balance catapults into chaos before his eyes. Like Humpty Dumpty, he fractures, and grace finally finds a way inside. Raleigh comes to grips with God's freedom to bestow favor:

> My God, thought Hayes now, what outrageous demands he'd made on Fortune. When at her indiscriminate whim, she could, and did, sweep away houses, love, children, position, health, and life, he'd asked for immunity. And he'd gotten it. Some rare, fragile, lucky—unparalleled lucky—fluke or grace had given him, for no earthly reason, like surprise presents, everything, absolutely everything, he'd thought he earned, and sustained by his own will, and deserved, and deserved *more*. Whereas, in fact, the world, or its creator, had not the slightest obligation to him at all.... It was not obliged to put the much-remarked petals on the lilies, nor keep its famous eye on the sparrow, nor reward Raleigh W. Hayes for his

virtue, nor punish sinners for their vice, nor protect the innocent, nor judge the guilty.

God stripped away all semblance of order in Raleigh's life. People stepped on all the lines, messing up the masking tape and acting as though Raleigh's elaborate box of safety did not even exist. Simultaneously they tormented him with a deluge of noisy, rowdy love. God grabbed Raleigh's chin and shifted his gaze upward, wooing him with grace.

Grace means that God does not require us to earn love and, conversely, is not hindered by our unworthiness. Through the sufficient work of Christ, grace expands to enfold the entirety of our lives. We rest in the assurance of reconciliation with God for eternity because God chooses to love.

Like Raleigh, we must acknowledge both the *need* for favor *and* its unmerited nature. This humility exposes the deep-seated pride of self-righteousness and self-sufficiency. We come to experience God as the strength and portion heralded by the Old Testament psalmist: "You who live in the shelter of the Most High, who abide in the shadow of the Almighty, will say to the LORD, 'My refuge and my fortress; my God, in whom I trust.'" God alone can grant your next breath.

A poem from Madeleine L'Engle presents an exquisite portrait of God's gracious love. *Behold!* she entreats. *Hear, taste, see, smell the grace of God!*

• • • • • stop a moment

L'Engle's poem speaks of God's grace in the minute details of our days: fingers finding the sound of Bach, the whisper of grass growing, the smell of a baby, the salt of tears. How do you see grace in the small corners of life? Where does God meet you with favor that comforts your soul? What would you add to the poem if we asked you to write a few more lines?

After the Saturday Liturgy at Montfort
by Madeleine L'Engle

O taste, and see, how gracious the Lord is:

taste! taste and see

bread, fresh and hot from the oven,

spring water, bubbling up from the rocks on a hot day,

tears, salt and warm as I kiss away a child's hurt,

wine, shared, as the cup is passed,

tears, salt and bitter, my tears, hot with pain,

lips, tender and loving, comforting and healing,

O taste! taste and see.

O hear, and see, how gracious the Lord is:

hear! hear and see

the thunder of his joy as galaxies fling across the Cosmos,

the whisper of grass growing,

the voice of the beloved,

my own fingers finding the sound of Bach.

the greeting of friends,

laughter and sharing and song,

and the words of healing bringing new life.

O hear! hear and see.

O sniff, smell and see, how gracious the Lord is:

smell! sniff and see

the salt of the ocean and the rush of wind,

the sweet puckering smell of grapes being pressed for wine,

the odour of rising dough, promise of bread,
and oh, did you know you can recognize your own baby by
    its smell?
and those you love most dearly, too, the unique, original
    smell of flesh
created—like flaming suns, like the smallest hydrogen
    atom—
to the honour and glory of his Name
O sniff! smell and see.

O feel, and see, how gracious the Lord is:
feel! touch and see
    bread in your fingers; feel it, bite and swallow;
    and wine, warm and living, spreading its fire through
        your body;
    take my hand, let me take yours, touch,
    so moves the Spirit through us—O touch me, heal me,
        hold me—
    God moves through our fingers—
    Reach out, touch the sun
    do not be afraid, O swallower of flame
    for this fire burns in order to give life.

Feel! Touch and see
    how gracious the Lord is!
Taste, hear, smell, feel and see
    how gracious the Lord is!

possibility

The idea of possibility lingers in the word "grace." The Holy Spirit works to bring about real change in the space God provides. Barbara Brown Taylor saw salvation where God moves in our lives:

> Salvation is a word for the divine spaciousness that comes to human beings in all the tight places where their lives are at risk, regardless of how they got there or whether they know God's name. Sometimes it comes as an extended human hand and sometimes a bolt from the blue, but either way it opens a door in what looked for all the world like a wall. This is the way of life, and God alone knows how it works.

A colleague comes to you after a botched project, expecting an onslaught of anger. You shock him with, "I know the deadlines were brutal. Let's grab some coffee, look things over and see what we can work out." Proffering undeserved, unmerited favor in God's name honors the image of God in our fellow human beings as we open a door that seemed like a wall.

Grace moves in the fractures and fissures of our lives to heal and restore. Like a fluid being injected into a cracked rock formation, grace flows into the voids caused by the pressures and stresses and heat of this world. Its presence brings the hope of wholeness once again.

A church in our town has a reputation for being wild about grace. The doors open wide for all kinds of people to come in from the cold, like the Statue of Liberty for the broken, tired and downtrodden who yearn to breathe freedom. We hear people talk about "that grace church" as if that label presents a problem. Some really messy people go to that church. Really messy people go to any church or avoid all churches; this grace church just happens to let it all hang out in the light of day.

You might advise caution in offering grace to others. One must be prudent, you know. Give people an inch and they will take a mile. Maybe people will presume upon grace. Maybe people will make mistakes. But at some point you must relinquish the role of sergeant-at-arms. Each of us will presume upon grace. Each of us will make mistakes.

The Spirit leads us to rise above an economy of scarcity when dispensing grace. Accepting grace from God and hoarding it under our mattress—saving it for a bad day when we need an extra measure—goes against the nature of grace as love given away. Maybe we fear we will run out. We parcel it out to those we deem most deserving. We forget the supply flows endlessly, and none of us deserves it. Grace flows through us and changes us as it moves out from us and into the lives of others. The sphere expands.

Grace moves in the fractures and fissures

Dietrich Bonhoeffer grieved over the stunted experience of community often found among people who profess to follow Christ. "The final break-through to fellowship does not occur, because, though they have fellowship with one another as believers and as devout people, they do not have fellowship as the undevout, as sinners. . . . Many Christians are unthinkably horrified when a real sinner is suddenly discovered among the righteous."

Strangely, people look askance at a church because of its congregation's affection for grace. Where better for such a reputation to reside? Jesus asked for all who are burdened and heavy-laden to come and receive rest. Jesus did not tell everyone to stop by the carwash on the way in, get cleaned up and then drive by for a blessing.

Rarely will anyone die for a righteous person—though perhaps for a good person someone might actually dare to die. But God proves his love for us in that while we still were sinners Christ died for us. Romans 5

Doug Pagitt, a pastor known for hospitality, speaks of churches where you can belong as you become, like that grace church. No requirement exists to become before you can belong. Grace erases lines that function as tightropes for people to walk. Grace means we love others while they are still sinners, just as Christ loves us.

Maybe grace for the sinner is an easy concept to grasp. You breathe one more time without being zapped. God must be gracious. But what about grace for the saint? Is it possible to need less grace as you progress up the ladder of spiritual maturity? If you are really close to perfection and not using your full allotment of grace, maybe you can leave some behind for the sinners?

> The opposite of sin is grace, not virtue.
> Philip Yancey

Matthew 20 records Christ's parable of the laborers. An employer hires one laborer early in the morning, promising to pay a denarius for the day's work. He hires another an hour later. Throughout the day, the employer hires more laborers, up until the last hour of the workday. He tells each one that he will pay "what is right."

All the laborers gather to receive their payment as the sun begins to set. The employer first pays the last man hired. That man receives a denarius. Each laborer receives a denarius. The first men hired protest in outrage. They demand to know why the last hired received the same pay: "These last men have worked only one hour, and you have made them equal to us who have borne the burden and the scorching heat of the day." Maybe they threatened to sue over fair-wage practices.

The employer answers, "Is it not lawful for me to do what I wish with what is my own? Or is your eye envious because I am generous? So, the last shall be first, and the first shall be last."

Grace reigns as the distinctive mark of God's love, and that mark often seems unfair. Yancey called it the scandalous mathematics of grace, going on to say:

> Grace is not about finishing first or last; it is about not counting....We risk missing the story's point: that God dispenses gifts, not wages. None of us gets paid according to merit, for none of us comes close to satisfying God's requirements for a perfect life. If paid on the basis of fairness, we would all end up in hell....In the bottom-line realm of ungrace, some workers deserve more than others; in the realm of grace, the word *deserve* does not even apply.

The accounts do not balance. One plus one does not equal two. Grace is freely extended, unmerited favor. Unmerited cannot be quantified, so a mathematical equation does not help. Christ abolished the ledger once and for all in our redemption. Keeping accounts has no place in God's economy.

Novelist Flannery O'Connor wrote about the gritty reality of the human condition. Her stories revealed the hard prejudices of the South. Unflinching portraits of sin and grace made up the backbone of her work.

In O'Connor's short story "Revelation," Mrs. Turpin sits in the doctor's office with her husband, Claud. She looks around, compares herself to each person in the room and concludes she is superior to all of them. She thanks God that she was created as a woman with a good disposition. She thanks God that she was *not* made like any of the other people. She remains completely blind to her pride.

As the story ends, Mrs. Turpin leans on the fence of her pigpen. She has a blinding vision of the end of her life as the sun sets in front of her. A bridge spans from earth to heaven. A throng of people cross over on their way to glory. To Mrs. Turpin's great surprise, all the people she labeled unworthy— the white trash, the blacks and the people without a lick of sense—march in front of her, shining in cleanliness, some in white robes, all shouting and dancing in joy.

And bringing up the end of the procession was a tribe of people whom she recognized at once as those who, like herself and Claud, had always had a little of everything and the God-given wit to use it right. She leaned forward to observe them closer. They were marching behind the others with great dignity, accountable as they had always been for good order and common sense and respectable behavior. They alone were on key. Yet she could see by their shocked and altered faces that even their virtues were being burned away.

· · · · · stop a moment

What is the best you have to offer? What do you bring to the table for God? Your best qualities. When people gather, they say, "Let Rachel head the Fall Funfest because she has so much energy." Or "Let Bill plan the service project because he can organize anything." Or "Let Carol do the budget because she can squeeze blood out of a turnip." What would people say about you? Write those qualities or attributes below. Think of the strengths you might write on a job application or to be considered for a volunteer position at church or in the community. Go ahead. Write all those strengths down.

_____   _____

_____   _____

_____   _____

_____   _____

Now imagine that we ask you to rip out your list (oh, no!) and follow us outside. We gather around a fire pit where flames rise from the coals. We ask you to put the list into the fire. We throw our lists in with yours. There we are, the best of us, beginning to blacken at the edges before bursting into flame. We stand together, watching the papers burn. To ashes.

Now you see what O'Connor meant when Mrs. Turpin saw even her virtues burned away. The parable of the laborers taught that the last was first, and the first last. Grace means we come to God holding nothing—neither sin nor virtue—in our hands.

· · · · ·

If then there is any encouragement in Christ, any consolation from love, any sharing in the Spirit, any compassion and sympathy, make my joy complete: be of the same mind, having the same love, being in full accord and of one mind. Do nothing from selfish ambition or conceit, but in humility regard others as better than yourselves. Let each of you look not to your own interests, but to the interests of others. Let the same mind be in you that was in Christ Jesus. Philippians 2

maturity

Our ability to be conduits of grace forms in community. In the previous chapter, we highlighted the Holy Spirit's use of community as a primary agent of change in our transformation. The process of learning both to receive and to extend grace requires that we unlearn the rhythms of self-directed lives. We begin to give priority to opening doors and tearing down walls as we are at the disposal of grace for God's purposes. The Spirit uses other people to spur our affection for God's gracious love as we mature from loving poorly to loving well.

We commit the sin of ungrace in disobedience to the law of love. We sin by withholding grace even though we have known grace. We act like young siblings brushing by each other in the hallway.

"Hey, you touched me!"

"Sooorry!"

"Who put you in charge of the hallway?"

"Why are you touching my hairbrush?"

"Because you are touching my towel!"

"I called the shower first."

"You were first yesterday!"

Fouls run rampant. We careen into each other in the hallways of life. We love poorly as we trespass against each other so willingly.

So what does grace look like as you practice this life with God? Taylor wrote that "salvation happens every time someone with a key uses it to open a door he could lock instead." What keys do you hold? Do you open doors or lock them?

The soap in the shower is down to a sliver. The toilet roll is bare. Your spouse or roommate or child knows how much that bothers you. How many times do you have to ask for a mite of consideration for such things as soap and toilet paper? How hard can that be? They fail to replace the article because they intend to drive you crazy. You must track them down and explain this one more time! Or you could put out new soap and new toilet paper and never say a word.

When we view spiritual maturity as increasing delight in the glory of God, loving lavishly becomes the holiest action we take. The vast majority of the time, we have the opportunity to extend grace in the daily details like soap and toilet paper. Loving lavishly requires persistent, patient grace in the nooks and crannies of life. There are moments when God calls us to grand gestures such as postponing or giving up your dreams to send a child off to college or caring for an elderly parent without an end in sight or even forgiving an atrocity to make way for new life to bloom.

Maturity in grace involves a self-forgetting that moves to be gracious without calculated gain. It provides hope to fractured lives by championing possibility and inspiring dreams. Maturity in grace believes the best in others and wishes the best for others. It acknowledges that only God has the full picture and foregoes any demand for a specific response or outcome. Maturity in grace treats love as the gospel and does not keep track of how many evangelistic tracts you passed out this week.

· · · · · a story from Bob

In one of my seminary classes, we discussed the concept of gender and explored the participation of women and men in the church. My own journey on the topic led me to cross many of the lines my students had drawn. I pushed hard against a constricting and reductive box and encouraged expansive thinking. One student vehemently contested my arguments in one class. Mark vented in the parking lot with other students during the break. I could hear him all the way from the building. He never returned to class that day.

I prayed hard that the Spirit of God would help me love well in this situation. I sent Mark an email suggesting we meet before the next class. Embarrassed by his outburst, he accepted the invitation. When we met, I got a picture of what Mark's days look like. He ministers widely in this city. He preaches, teaches, pastors—he does it all. He also has several very young children. Add attending seminary to that list, and you have an exhausted, stressed individual.

I asked Mark about his reaction to the class. He explained his fears about stepping on the lines. We talked about the process of learning. I suggested that he was so tired and stretched so thin that he did not have the capacity to encounter a radically new idea. Mark nodded wearily. We did not agree on everything, but we enjoyed an open and healthy dialogue. We had the privilege of watching the Spirit's work of grace restore our fellowship. God's glory reigned.

         *   *   *   *   *

Your spouse answers a question sharply. Your mother laments that your new white sofa will be a magnet for dirt. The store cashier makes a turtle look like a speed demon. Your boss loses the report you delivered. As you consider your response, you have a choice: for grace or against grace. The choice comes at what feels like a huge personal price. You love the other because you reflect what and how God loves.

We may have no idea what road the person standing before us has walked. Your mother may have never had the luxury of a new couch. Or she might simply be unaccustomed to giving a compliment because she has rarely heard one. The cashier may work three jobs, take care of two kids, and have a splitting headache. Or he might simply be slow. Your boss may have stayed up all night working on sales figures for her boss. Or she might simply be disorganized.

Grace moves us to love people even when they disappoint us and sin against us. It moves us to love people even when circumstances are ugly and messy. Gracious love can feel hard and often unfair. Others may not deserve our love. Others may not earn our love. God could say the same about us.

There is no need to hoard God's love or parcel it out with caution. Love, as the first fruit of the Spirit, transforms our affection so that, in the words of Frederick Buechner, "little by little compassionate love begins to change from a moral exercise, from a matter of gritting our teeth and doing our good deed for the day, into a joyous, spontaneous, self-forgetting response to the most real aspect of all reality, which is that the world is holy because God made it and so is every one of us as well."

Let no evil talk come out of your mouths, but only what is useful for building up, as there is need, so that your words may give grace to those who hear. And do not grieve the Holy Spirit of God, with which you were marked with a seal for the day of redemption. Put away from you all bitterness and wrath and anger and wrangling and slander, together with all malice, and be kind to one another, tenderhearted, forgiving one another, as God in Christ has forgiven you. Therefore be imitators of God, as beloved children, and live in love, as Christ loved us and gave himself for us, a fragrant offering and sacrifice to God. Ephesians 4 and 5

· · · · · stop a moment

Try on these additional images of what embodied love might look like as we are conduits for God's grace.

Forgiving an obvious slight	Writing funny letters
Playing catch endlessly	Sending care packages
Offering a ride	Showing up without a reason
Preparing a meal	Listening to violin practice
Lending your jacket	Holding tiny jellied hands
Wiping elderly drool	Massaging gnarled feet
Complimenting a colleague	Laughing until tears flow

How have you been the space of grace for someone this week? How have you seen God's grace extended by others toward you? Can you add one or two images in the margin?

· · · · ·

We fulfill our fully human purpose as we celebrate the glorious beauty of God's gracious love. That love finds its transforming power in the next two topics we cover. Forgiving love, in "Gift," forfeits the right to revenge, opening the way to restoration. Sacrificial love, in "Fool," requires putting your life at God's disposal with gladness. Both come only through the Holy Spirit shifting our affection toward the character of God.

May you frolic in the beams
of God's mystifying love for you
and fling that love with abandon
upon everyone in your world to the glory of God.

Let grace run amok.

LifeSpace

chapter nine

gift

(gift), noun.
Anything voluntarily transferred from one person to
another without compensation; a present.

Christmas nears as we write this chapter. Catalogs and advertising flyers fill mailboxes. Just arrived! The newest toy for your tot! Slippers for Dad are on sale! Every teen covets this computer!

Sincere young Christians wear "Jesus is the Reason for the Season" sweatshirts in a valiant attempt to redeem the hubbub and hoopla. We bring shoeboxes full of school supplies to the church, with five dollars attached for postage to an orphan. We pick paper angels off a tree to buy coats for an immigrant family. Our pumpkin pie recipes double to provide for the elderly couple down the block.

We give gifts—presents bestowed freely, transferred voluntarily without any expectation of being compensated. The orphan will not send money to pay for the school supplies. A hand-painted note of thanks might pleasantly surprise us. The pumpkin pie will not come back. Prudence tells us to use a disposable pie plate.

The gift of grace is often wrapped in forgiveness, delivering undeserved, unmerited favor. This present can be the hardest to extend to our fellow human beings. Pride and hurt threaten to rip off the paper and stomp on the package. The contents are infinitely fragile and irreplaceable. Forgiveness brings the gift of a new beginning to the carnage of human relationships. It is the gift of Life.

· · · · · stop a moment

We define the idea of a present broadly. Think about how you would more specifically define the gift of forgiveness. Grab a pen or pencil again. Look at the five pods of description that follow. A definition of forgiveness might include some of these words. We want you to approach the concept from a new perspective.

We filled in a few blanks to help get the creative juices flowing. Revenge has the acrid, dead smell of wet ashes. Restoration feels as light and soft as lamb's fleece. Debt colors your world overdrawn red. Freedom tastes like wild, juicy blackberries. Injustice screams in frustration.

Give yourself time and permission to be reflective here. You may find it helpful to close your eyes as you consider the words. What comes to mind? An answer key cannot be found in the back of the book. Play with the ideas a bit.

The Aroma of...

revenge	*wet ashes*
affection	
surrender	
miracle	

The Texture of...

retaliation	
favor	
guilt	
restoration	*lamb's fleece*

The Color of...

grace	
debt	*red*
release	
anger	

The Taste of...

mercy	
sin	
freedom	*wild blackberries*
resentment	

The Sound of...

pardon	
injustice	*screaming*
reconciliation	
brokenness	

Now look at the picture drawn by your words. What if you sort words like "mercy," "restoration" and "pardon" to one side of the page and "guilt," "anger" and "revenge" to the other? Which feels more like life? Like breath?

• • • • •

definition

Your local bookstore offers aisles filled with self-help titles promising the perfect formula for forgiving the hurt in your life. Each author posits a definition of forgiveness that is highlighted as unique. The words may change, but the basic elements are usually the same.

A good definition seems to require, at minimum, the recognition of a precipitating act of injury, the free choice to turn back anger, and a positive change of status for the relationship. Author Herbert Lockyer defined forgiveness in this way:

> The word forgiveness means to discharge, dismiss, aquit, let loose from, to remit a debt or sin, to pardon. It also implies giving up an inward feeling of injury or resentment, the removal of a feeling of anger, and restoration of a feeling of favor and affection.

People stick incorrect labels on forgiveness, as if to tame it. Forgiveness is not tolerance. Tolerance can focus on the good in a situation without dealing with the evil. Forgiveness recognizes that unjust injury actually occurred. You can forgive something you should never consider tolerating. A woman with an abusive husband may well forgive him in mercy, but she may also leave the marriage as she refuses to tolerate the abuse. Rightly so.

Forgiveness is not forgetting. You can sincerely forgive while still remembering. Space exists between our memories and the choices we make in the present. A movie about the Truth and Reconciliation proceedings in South Africa told the story of one man's road to forgiving his torturers. When he approved amnesty for his oppressors, the man told a fellow sufferer, "We still have the right to say that it hurt."

Mass graves from genocide are often marked with the words "Never again." Memory instructs the future of relationships between human beings. We simultaneously remember both the reality of evil and the determination to forgive.

Finally, forgiveness is not understanding. To understand all is not to forgive all. Conversely, to forgive all is not necessarily to understand all. In most conflicts, truth is elusive. The opportunity for restoration may never come to pass if you wait to agree on all the facts.

True forgiveness shifts our affection from wrath toward benevolence. This transformative turn reflects God's loving purpose in redemption. "Every perfect gift is from above, from the Father of Lights, from the Lord of Love." This musical chorus echoes scripture, pointing us to forgiveness as gift. God loved us and forgave our sins while we were yet sinners. Out of that forgiveness, we extend the gift to others.

motive

The Bible shows humanity crying out to the Lord again and again. "Have mercy on us, O Lord!" "Turn your wrath, O Lord, and forgive our iniquity!" "Remember your steadfast and merciful love, O Lord!" This cacophony of pleading for forgiveness and mercy starts in Genesis and continues through Revelation. It sounds like a cat up a tree, there by its own volition but crying for help out of the mess of trouble.

It makes you wonder why God chose the path of forgiveness in dealing with human beings—a bucketful of heartache since the beginning of time. We prostitute ourselves with other lovers.

Idols of marriage and jobs and safety and independence and a hundred other things leave us wailing, bereft in dark alleyways. We presume upon God's goodness with expectations of pleasant pastures. God could justifiably choose to rid the earth of our presence without a backward glance.

In forgiving human sin, God reclaims the purpose of creation, determining that divine glory will shine. That which is the greatest good for all—peace and restoration—brings fame to the name of God. Jeremiah declared God's gracious intent to restore the Israelites from their idolatrous ways:

> I will cleanse them from all the guilt of their sin against me, and I will forgive all the guilt of their sin and rebellion against me. And this city shall be to me a name of joy, a praise and a glory before all the nations of the earth who shall hear of all the good that I do for them.

Our relationship with God does not operate under a contract in which both sides must fulfill the terms or the deal is null and void. God initiated the covenant of love and has pledged to sustain the covenant as the source of Life. Our alienation from God ended forever at the resurrection of the crucified Christ. The apostle Peter celebrated the life-giving result in 1 Peter 1: "By his great mercy he has given us a new birth into a living hope through the resurrection of Jesus Christ from the dead, and into an inheritance that is imperishable, undefiled, and unfading."

Being the forgiven can be humbling. To accept God's forgiveness means we acknowledge our need to be forgiven.

Being the "forgiven" can be humbling

We struggle with the insinuation of needing forgiveness—are we really that bad?—and there being no merit in all our best efforts to shine—what about some credit coming our way?

Being the forgiven means unequivocally naming our lesser loves as "sin," an affront to the holy God. The prophet Hosea called Israel to assume the humble stance of the forgiven in Hosea 14. "Take words with you and return to the LORD; say to him, 'Take away all guilt; accept that which is good, and we will offer the fruit of our lips. Assyria will not save us; we will not ride upon horses; we will say no more, "Our God," to the work of our hands. In you the orphan finds mercy.'"

Owning our sin requires we be real versus imaginary sinners—a distinction made by Martin Luther. By admitting the need for forgiveness, we stop defending ourselves with valiant, self-righteous oratories. Jesus rebuked such vanity in the story of the Pharisee and tax collector in Luke 18. The Pharisee reminds us of Mrs. Turpin in Flannery O'Connor's story of burning virtues.

> The Pharisee, standing by himself, was praying thus, "God, I thank you that I am not like other people: thieves, rogues, adulterers, or even like this tax collector. I fast twice a week; I give a tenth of all my income." But the tax collector, standing far off, would not even look up to heaven, but was beating his breast and saying, "God, be merciful to me, a sinner!" I tell you, this man went down to his home justified rather than the other; for all who exalt themselves will be humbled, but all who humble themselves will be exalted.

Philip Yancey said it simply: "Grace means there is nothing I can do to make God love me more, and nothing I can do to make God love me less." What a humbling place to be. Our gracious God considers that we are "but flesh, a wind that passes and does not come again." God has compassion on us and remembers our beginning in the dirt. In order to *extend* forgiveness in the name of God, we must first *accept* forgiveness in the name of God.

Read over the passages of scripture in this section. Read them as a prayer to God, praising the steadfast love of your Redeemer. Thank God for the gift of forgiveness in Christ. Ask the Holy Spirit for the humility to appear empty-handed before the throne of God. Take a moment of silence to rest in God's grace.

• • • • •

resurrection

Did you ever get a big chocolate bunny in your basket on Easter morning? You fully intended to eat the whole bunny by yourself, ignoring your mother's warning that it would make you sick. The one time you offered your brother a bite, he bit the bunny's head off. Sharing Easter candy can be dangerous that way.

The Easter gift of resurrected life is meant to be shared as we embody the gift of God's grace to others. All humanity needs forgiveness as a portal to new life. The gift begins at God's initiative and continues through our willingness to be life-giving agents of grace. The Catholic priest and enduring servant Henri Nouwen understood sharing the Easter gift:

> Forgiveness is the name of love practiced among people who love poorly. The hard truth is that all of us love poorly. We need to forgive and be forgiven every day, every hour—unceasingly. That is the great work of love among the fellowship of the weak that is the human family.

The hard truth is we all love poorly. Humans commit horrific sins against each other. We extinguish human life through neglect, abuse and murder. Conflict brings destitution and destruction at all levels of society, with a particular burden on the weak and oppressed. We trespass widely and wildly against each other.

There should be operating manuals on how to be human together. On many days, the best we accomplish is simply staying out of each other's way. Seven steps to forgiveness seem like a thousand when you stare at a bank account decimated by a dishonest employee or the grave of your child killed by a drunk driver. This topic is not easy. Only through the gracious provision of the Spirit of God can we hope to love others well while both we and they love poorly.

We interviewed our friend Bernadette for this book. She lived through genocide, and we wanted to talk about the aftermath of those atrocities and the process of forgiveness. Before she addressed the topic at hand, Bernadette told us about a recent trip abroad to her father's house. She ended up riding in a car with a seat that tried to eject her whenever she sat down. The car door had no hinges, so the driver lifted the door on and off the frame to allow passengers to disembark. We laughed with Bernadette at the picture of her jostling down a dirt trail in this rattletrap.

The father had abandoned Bernadette's family long before the war. He left his wife and eight children to move to the next village, taking Bernadette's aunt as his second wife. The father had twelve more kids with his new wife. Both villages ostracized the new family. They lived in a tiny metal shack, crowded on top of each other, with stars shining through the gaping holes in the tin roof at night. Bernadette's mother raised her children like many women in war-torn countries, barely surviving.

"I did not want to continue to cut that wound, never allowing it to heal," Bernadette told us. This past year, taking Celestin's and her eldest daughter along, she traveled from the United States to Africa and down that dirt trail to her father's house. "The Holy Spirit moved me to go." Bernadette extended her arms in peace. "My aunt told everyone that Christians live like people who are in heaven, because I called her 'Mom.'"

Bernadette's faithfulness to the leading of God's Spirit began a healing process in a community wider than just her family.

"The village elders came to the house while I was there. They said they had not visited my father in fifteen years. Because I came, they came. People from all over the area watched me reconcile with my father.

"My visit outraged my brothers and sisters. My father did many bad things to our family. He tried to take all our land and money, leaving my mother with nothing. He did not show any sorrow for his actions against us. But I wanted to be healed. There is still a scar, but it is no longer on my heart. Forgiveness is an opportunity to begin again. Before I went, my father thought of me as one who hates him. Now he and my aunt call my daughter 'The one whose mother cares for me.'"

"I still do not trust my father. He has not changed. But our daughter sees a new future. My aunt sees a new future. Maybe someday my brothers and sisters will join me. Maybe someday my father will repent and find his own forgiveness.

Celestin told of how forgiveness creates an umbrella of grace over more than just the immediate relationship. "An old friend's family was involved in killing my family during the genocide. He and I reconciled and are now closer than ever before. My forgiveness extends beyond my friend to his entire family and everyone connected to him. It even extends to the physical land where the evil took place.

"When I miss my father, the anger and hate have an opportunity to come back. I have to apply forgiveness again and again to the memory. There is no remedy for hatred other than forgiveness."

As much as forgiveness is a gift, it is also a discipline. You must remember *that* forgiveness occurred. You embrace the resurrection miracle from God over and over. The reality of the past remains while you choose to move forward into a different future together.

Whether in the evil of mass genocide or in a family story of abandonment or in the nicks and scrapes of daily life, we love each other poorly. Forgiveness brings the gospel of resurrection to life, with mercy anew every morning.

Through the Spirit, we come to share God's motive in forgiveness: the reclamation of God's glory through the restoration of fully human life. Roped together, what tears me down and brings death, tears you down and brings death. What breathes new life into me, breathes new life into you. Forgiveness, both for the one who forgives and for the forgiven, is a self-giving for the sake of love.

As forgiveness is a gift, it is also a sacrifice. You give up death for life and callousness for empathy. Jesus blessed sacrificial love in the Sermon of the Mount. Blessed are those who can be gentle in the face of harshness, merciful in the face of injury and peaceful in the face of enmity.

Miroslav Volf, a theologian who survived an ethnic war between Serbians and Croatians, wrote of a "theology of embrace" versus a "theology of exclusion":

> The will to give ourselves to others and "welcome" them, to readjust our identities to make space for them, is prior to any judgment about others, except that of identifying them in their humanity. The will to embrace . . . transcends the moral mapping of the social world into "good" and "evil."

We cannot sort human beings into neat columns of evil and good. We join hands as fellow sinners with divided hearts, dark and light coexisting in each of us.

● ● ● ● ● a story from Joni

Two relationships in my life ended abruptly and badly—one at age 25 and the other at age 45, almost twenty years to the day. Two different friendships torn asunder remain in disrepair. The details do not matter at this juncture. Suffice it to say that I had a story, and each of them had a story, and parting seemed like the only path open at the time.

I eventually lost track of the first person. Work took us to different cities; life took us to different worlds. I think about our friendship when I see old pictures of us at the ocean or at the company summer outing. I still wonder what really happened to cause such anger between us.

The more recent rift occurred with a friend here in my city. I ducked behind a pillar in order to avoid running into her the week after our parting. Since then, our paths have not crossed. The day will come. I steel myself for it even now.

I play the scripts of my last encounters with these two people over in my mind, my lines and their lines. My own form of revisionist history often takes over, making myself the hero and them the villains. The passage of time affords a false clarity that belies the confusion of what really happened.

I wrap these events of unforgiveness in a gold cloth of grace. My prayer covers them, asking the Holy Spirit to reveal the truth about my contribution to the pain. I want to be willing to make the first move if ever such an opportunity arises. I want the courage to step out from behind the pillar.

Little bits of scar tissue form when forgiveness—either forgiving or asking to be forgiven or both at the same time—is postponed. Like a respiratory disease, the lungs lose their elasticity for breath. I want to breathe expansively by claiming the peace that comes in reconciled, healthy relationships, where I fulfill my human purpose to love as God loves.

I am not there yet. My prayer today is that I am willing to be willing.

•　　•　　•　　•　　•

Professor and poet Marilyn Chandler McEntyre wrote of the opportunity to live the gospel in the hard places of forgiveness: "So how do I love you now? Badly. Intermittently. Sometimes grudgingly. But I know that we, you and I, are here to help one another work out our salvation, perhaps with fear and trembling. And so I must be grateful for you—not for the evil that you do, which is not mine to judge—but for the ways in which you, my enemies, are an occasion of grace."

In Matthew 18, Jesus used a parable to answer the disciples' question about who will be the greatest in heaven. He told of an unforgiving servant, who asked forgiveness of an onerous debt from his master and then had a fellow slave thrown into prison for owing a pittance. The master responded with wrath, "I forgave you all that debt because you pleaded with me. Should you not have had mercy on your fellow slave, as I had mercy on you?"

The gift of forgiveness brings the gospel to life. Breathing room opens up as the self-giving of Christ becomes our own self-giving. Christ operates out of an economy of abundance in grace versus an economy of scarcity. We dip our ladles in the deep well of grace, offering a cool drink to a parched world.

process

So how to begin? While formulas can be informative here, forgiveness is and will remain a miraculous work of the Holy Spirit. You learn to forgive in fits and starts. Just when you think you have it down, teetering on pride over the whole thing, someone comes crashing through your defenses. Forgiveness stays wily and wooly that way.

Are you committed to embrace or exclusion? As we say in "Rope," you will commune either well or poorly, but you will commune. Can you make space for people to grow in their fully human purpose of glorifying God and delighting in that glory? The Spirit transforms our affection to love restoration more than we love our individual rights. The generative, creative power of love heals our relationships through the balm of benevolence. Lewis Smedes writes:

> When we forgive we come as close as a human being can to the essential divine act of creation, for we create a new beginning out of the past pain that never had a right to exist in the first place. We create healing for the future by changing a past that had no possibility in it for anything but sickness and death.

There is a progression in forgiveness. It takes courage from the Spirit of God to move toward reconciliation. Much easier to harbor our grudges and to stoke the embers of hate. The humility to make the first move constitutes transcendent sacrifice. This is true whether you bestow the gift or hope to be the recipient.

After a nasty split in our church congregation, people on both sides of the conflict were waiting for an apology. But forgiveness, as a gift of grace, cannot be conditioned on repentance. While apologies are certainly beneficial, forgiveness does not demand compensation.

Forgiveness also supplants the right to revenge. We acquiesce to God's role as judge. We act as instruments of God's love while being satisfied that God controls the outcome. God's justice and presence under gird what Volf called "costly acts of nonretaliation." These acts become "a seed from which the fragile fruit of Pentecostal peace grows."

Forgiveness requires the patience of time and effort in reconciling relationships. Perhaps you come around the corner of the grocery aisle and run into someone's cart. "Please excuse me!" you exclaim if you have any manners at all. "Oh, no problem!" the person responds if he has any manners at all. That is the easy example. It only gets harder from here.

I was at a large gathering for men (the sponsoring organization to remain unnamed) where the speaker focused on the sin of racism. He asked each of us to locate a person of another color somewhere in the crowd and confess our sin directly to him. Even in that huge gathering, finding such a person presented a challenge. It also seemed a little odd to grab a total stranger for an impromptu confession.

The Anglo guy next to me honed in on an African-American man down one row. He prepared to pour out his heart.

"Sometimes I've been kind of racist."

The black man answered, "OK."

They both stood there awkwardly for a moment, then shook hands and parted.

When my seatmate returned to my side, he exclaimed, "Man, I feel better!"

The whole exercise mocked the hard work of forgiveness between human beings. You cannot take an entire lifetime of racism and wrap it up in one sentence that did not even qualify as an apology. Nice that my seatmate felt better. Totally inconsequential to the real point of forgiveness, but nice.

● ● ● ● ●

We give our retreat participants a pile of white river rocks. Each rock is about the size of an egg. The people spread out around the retreat grounds to reflect on the place of forgiveness in their lives. We ask them to write an event of unforgiveness on each rock. Maybe it is the name of a person or a date or a place or a word that reminds them of a conversation. Perhaps they need forgiveness or have withheld forgiveness. No one reveals their rocks to the group, so the time of reflection remains anonymous.

When we call the group back together, you can almost see the expectation on their faces. They stand ready to march en masse over to the nearby river and throw all their rocks into the rushing water at our command. The perfect solution! Retreats bring such grand gestures. All those events forgiven in one fell swoop. Convenient, but not realistic.

Each participant receives a large square of shiny gold cloth. They wrap up their rocks, representing a swaddling in grace. We ask them to pray over the bundle for the next weeks and months. We suggest they periodically take the rocks out to see how the Spirit of God begins over time to transform their affection for forgiveness.

It would be nice if throwing the rocks in the river worked. Sometimes it does. More often, the Spirit works slowly to show us the greater love of peace and reconciliation over our own pride or hurt. Ethicist Lewis Smedes noted that "any movement toward *something like* reconciliation that begins with *something like* forgiveness is pushed along by *something like* repentance. These small signs and baby steps toward forgiveness constitute a reason for hope."

> Hardness the size of a boulder
> breaks into river rocks,
> then pebbles,
> then sand,
> finally turning to dust,
> blowing away with the wind.

Think about the sphere introduced in the first chapter. The practice of life with God has the sphere expanding outward as we become fully human. Just as Bernadette experienced, unforgiveness acts like scar tissue in its constriction of our growth. Imagine the half-opened sphere frozen into a block of ice. Expansion comes to a halt. Forgiveness works to free human lives from this imprisonment. Maybe through a slow melting. Or God might use a sledge hammer to shatter the hardness before your eyes.

・ ・ ・ ・ ・ **stop a moment**

What is your tolerance for forgiveness? Think about the skin of an elderly person. The skin feels crepe-y and fragile. One bump against the corner cabinet brings a wound or a bruise that takes weeks to heal. Infection lurks under the surface, waiting for the opportunity to blossom. Does this describe you? Easily slighted, with your pride on your shoulder to be jostled at the smallest bump? Do you keep long accounts that percolate on retold stories of perceived injury?

Do you freeze people into the narrative of your history as those who hurt you, with no opportunity to redefine themselves? Do you withhold forgiveness until the payment of acceptable words of repentance? That would not be a gift but rather a sales transaction. Do you have any idea where you would be today if God had such crepe-y elderly skin?

What is your tolerance for being the forgiven? Is that role a rare occurrence for you? Do you have the thick skin of an elephant with the texture of rubber tires? Could you be the person right now that someone has something against? What would you do about it? Even your apology can be a tool for manipulation. Perhaps you say, "I am sorry. Oh, I am sorry. Please, I am sorry." But you never accept responsibility for changing what makes you sorry and beginning anew?

● ● ● ● ●

A new attitude of forgiveness demonstrates willingness, through the power of the Spirit, to change your affection toward the other. A commitment to loving well evidences a new perspective of mutual dependence. Life expands with a new determination to begin, not with what and where you used to be, but with what and where you are now.

We cannot know how this chapter affects you. We would love to sit in rockers on a big porch somewhere, listening to your stories. You might tell us of the sweet tenderness that followed an excruciating apology. Or maybe the sphere trapped in ice paints a picture that comes too close to home. We believe that resurrection happens now but it requires a willingness to change. Maybe you could start by being willing to be willing. The Holy Spirit can work with that.

Forgiveness is primarily about hope. Without it, we all die. With it, we live eternal Life with a capital *L*. Forgiveness begins with God, flows through us and outward to others, remanding glory back to God. This gracious gift from the Spirit of God requires sacrifice on our part. Our next chapter, "Fool," further explores our role as sacrificial life-bearers of love.

And so the sphere expands.

I will heal their disloyalty;

I will love them freely,

for my anger has turned from them.

I will be like the dew to Israel;

he shall blossom like the lily,

he shall strike root like the forests of Lebanon.

His shoots shall spread out;

his beauty shall be like the olive tree,

and his fragrance like that of Lebanon.

They shall again live beneath my shadow,

they shall flourish as a garden,

they shall blossom like the vine,

their fragrance shall be like the wine of Lebanon.

Hosea 14

chapter ten

FO

OL

My life is at God's disposal
. . . with gladness.

A recent news story recounted the bittersweet arrival of a new baby girl. A diagnosis of cancer during the pregnancy brought unexpected, deathly complications. Failing rapidly, the mother elicited promises from her family that they would cherish her fourth child and only daughter. She spent the last months of the pregnancy comatose on life-support machines. The doctors delivered baby Veronica, held her above the mother's body and baptized her. The newborn cry was a torturous contrast to the abrupt silence of whirring machines as the mother died.

The practice of life with God calls us to pour out our lives for the sake of love over and over. Like Veronica's mother, we trade death for life. We put our mouth over another's and infuse resuscitating breath. The intensity and abandon of that love means the world may call us fools. The label must never dissuade us. Christ triumphantly goes before us, having endured the taunting jeers upon the cross. Fool! Fool!

> Where there is love,
> there will always be sacrifice.
> Mother Teresa

So there we have it—that word "sacrifice." Very unpopular in most circles today. It is so, well, intertwined. It means that our relationships pass beyond me telling you my story and you telling me your story and us making room for each other to have different stories and smiling back and forth to be nice. In sacrifice, my blood mixes with your blood. We prick our fingers and push them together to let the life intermingle. I am as thou art. If your blood gasps anemic from lack of oxygen, then mine gasps also. If my blood runs brilliant red with invigorating fresh air, so does yours.

Let us review where we have been in order to see where we are going in this chapter. This book begins with God as the expansive center of being. We celebrate the fully human purpose to glorify God and enjoy God forever. But all human beings turn from God through indifference, rebellion or attempts to control life with our own performance standards. Christ, the incarnated God, provides the way back. He affirms our humanity and draws us into a reality beyond ourselves.

The Holy Spirit transforms our affection for the person of God, resulting in a shift from the incurvature of self to an outward gaze. Our refrain changes from "Glory to me!" to "Glory to God!" Through the Spirit's work, we come to love what God loves and how God loves. In this we find our greatest joy. We see other human beings as objects of God's love and avenues used by the Spirit to expand our horizons. Grace reigns as the distinctive mark of God's love in our relationships with one another. It starts in forgiveness, the portal through which all of us walk into new life, redeemed for relationship with God. Grace continues in sacrifice, where all that is lost cannot compare to what is gained.

my
blood
mixes with
your
blood

Sacrifice means placing my life at God's disposal . . . with gladness. To magnify the perfections of God—perfect love, perfect justice, perfect joy—I lay down my entire being. On my best days, the Holy Spirit moves me to sacrifice graciously with an attitude that matches my actions. Other days, I cache anything of value in the back of the closet or under the mattress and hope no one finds it.

Gladness means I pour out my time, resources and efforts like sand in an hourglass and find delight in the loss. I may never hear "Thank you" or receive an engraved plaque. Living as hostage to others in the realm of grace: that is where the rubber meets the road on the fool's highway. I abandon my heart to love.

• • • • • stop a moment

We know a pastor in Cuba who comes to the United States each year for training. Marcos stays two weeks, reacquainting with old friends, drinking in the freedom of unguarded conversation and buying new shoes for his children. He then boards a plane to return to Cuba, closed for another year behind the steel door of Communism. He could ask for asylum and stay here. But Marcos says he must go back. "Everything I love is in Cuba: my family, my church, the people. God put me there. As hard as it is to get on that plane, the freedom I would have by staying here would mean nothing. I would not be living." Marcos' sacrificial love means he buys a roundtrip ticket.

What has sacrifice looked like in your life? Think of specific instances when you have put your life at the disposal of God for the service of others or when someone else has extended the favor to you. Maybe you tithe regularly at your church. Or your aunt let you live in her back room while you finished nursing school. Or you slept on the bathroom floor comforting a sick child all night last night. Give us three examples of sacrifice in your life: either by you or for you.

We brainstormed the following words in thinking of what humans might sacrifice. Stop a moment to read through them. Do any of these relate to your examples? What would you add to the list? Write the words down in the margin.

Freedom	Time	Control
Rights	Preferences	Success
Safety	Status	Dreams
Opportunity	Strength	Honor
Balance	Money	Reputation
Comfort	Privileges	Health

Circle the easiest thing for you to sacrifice out of all the words listed. Now circle the hardest. Why are they easy or hard for you? Perhaps you see safety as fleeting, so doing mission work among gangs in the inner city comes easy for you. But maybe you hang onto money because you remember putting cardboard in the bottom of your athletic shoes to cover the holes.

• • • • •

Shifting from the incurved love of self to the expansive love of God requires sacrifice. We acknowledge God as the center of life, admitting that the world does not revolve around us. Praise and thanksgiving for the greatness of God make it hard to extol the virtues of your own navel! We dance and sing and make fools of ourselves, exalting God's reputation without care for the world's standard of decorum.

The Old Testament sacrificial system recognized God's preeminent right to our affection. The priests offered the first fruits to God: the first sheaf of the harvest, the unblemished lamb, the powerful bull, the white dove. These represented the purest love of the creature for the Creator. An unbelieving observer surely thought the people foolish in their extravagance as the prime of their livelihood burned on an altar to God.

God still asks for the first fruits: of worship, of thanksgiving, of affection. Not because we earn divine love, but because God is the source of all things. Paul wrote of God's claim on our lives in Romans 14: "We do not live to ourselves, and we do not die to ourselves. If we live, we live to the Lord, and if we die, we die to the Lord; so then, whether we live or whether we die, we are the Lord's." When the next breath we take comes *from* God, everything following that breath belongs *to* God. Frederick Buechner states:

To worship God means to serve him. Basically there are two ways to do it. One way is to do things for him that he needs to have done—run errands for him, carry messages for him, fight on his side, feed his lambs, and so on. The other way is to do things for him that you need to do—sing songs for him, create beautiful things for him, give things up for him, tell him what's on your mind and in your heart, in general rejoice in him and make a fool of yourself for him the way lovers have always made fools of themselves for the one they love.

The love story of the prophet Hosea and the prostitute Gomer illustrates the sacrificial complexion of God's love. Hosea married Gomer, knowing her reputation of unfaithfulness. She continued to chase after other men. In a beautiful display of steadfast love, Hosea repeatedly retrieved her from deathly folly. God likewise perseveres in a persistent love for us.

> The entirety of
> my time, my space and my being
> is at God's disposal for love.

Through Jesus Christ the Son, God bestowed forgiveness once and for all in the ultimate offering of sacrificial love. Jesus declared in Mark 10, "For even the Son of Man did not come to be served, but to serve, and to give his life as a ransom for many." The pattern of Christ's cross and resurrection forges life out of death. We who were far off and alienated from God are brought near.

Christ calls us to follow this redemptive pattern. "I have said these things to you so that my joy may be in you, and that your joy may be complete. This is my commandment, that you love one another as I have loved you. No one has greater love than this, to lay down one's life for one's friends."

The apostle Paul preached the gospel of Christ throughout the land. He endured intense persecution and abuse, pouring himself out for the early church. In his letter to the Corinthians, Paul rejoiced in the glory brought to God through sacrifice:

> For while we live, we are always being given up to death for Jesus' sake, so that the life of Jesus may be made visible in our mortal flesh. So death is at work in us, but life in you. Yes, everything is for your sake, so that grace, as it extends to more and more people, may increase thanksgiving, to the glory of God. 2 Corinthians 4

Gracious sacrifice thumbs its nose at the world's expectation of tit-for-tat so you-scratch-my-back-I-scratch-your-back because karma-is-what-goes-around-comes-around. Sacrificing for the glory of God means you may never see a reward in human terms. Faithful obedience lays you in the path of transcendent joy as God delights in the reflection of perfect love. Henri Nouwen writes:

> This experience tells us that we can only love because we are born out of love, that we can only give because our life is a gift, and that we can only make others free because we are set free by Him whose heart is greater than ours. When we have found the anchor places for our lives in our own center, we can be free to let others enter into the space created for them and allow them to dance their own dance, sing their own song and speak their own language without fear. Then our presence is no longer threatening and demanding but inviting and liberating.

Sacrifice places your life at God's disposal ... with gladness. You lay your life down for the glory of God to shine, following the pattern of Christ's redeeming love. In this you find your greatest joy. What does it look like to play the fool for love? These signposts point the way.

You approach your fellow human beings in a stance of openness and acceptance. The crescent pose in the practice of yoga provides a good image here. In a deep lunge, you open your arms wide to the sky. Your back arches, exposing your chest and face. Palms turn up in a receptive manner. You choose vulnerability to the world around you.

We talk about being a "Here I am!" person or a "There you are!" person. Sacrifice means you make time to commune with real human beings in flesh and blood, expressing genuine interest in the details of their lives. The well-being of others matters to you. Human beings do not interrupt your life but rather bring color to your days. Some people have a face like a welcome mat and others like a sign that says "Beware of the dog." Which one are you?

It is a great loss if we greet every day with clenched hands stuffed with our own devices. We will never know what is out there waiting for us if we don't extend an empty hand to the world and wait for the wonder to happen. . . . We all have weapons to lay down and battles to call off before we can open up our hearts. It is a stance of surrender that we are talking about. Ultimately, hospitality is not about the table you set, or the driveway you plow. Hospitality is about preparing the holiest of holies. It is about the heart you make ready. Yours. Father Daniel Homan and Lonni Collins Pratt

 The Spirit of God enables us to sacrifice *with gladness*. Our affection is changed to love as God loves, allowing us to let go of clenched fists and fling love with joyful abandon. The physical aspect of sacrifice may come easily. A heart attitude of gladness can lag well

behind. Perhaps you sacrifice and immediately swell with pride at your magnanimous gesture. Or maybe you have the martyr's prim smile down pat. Attitude must combine with act to bring glory to God.

Joseph, the apostles' friend, received a new name in his service to the early church. They called him Barnabas, meaning "son of encouragement." He sold a field and gave all the proceeds to support the disciples' ministry. He laid the money at their feet. Imagine being thought of as an encouragement. You come alongside others in sacrifice for the joy of the Lord. That joy is contagious as it brings a breath of fresh air. Imagine being *renamed* Barnabas to reflect the real you.

To sacrifice is to make something holy by giving it away for love. Buechner

 Sacrifice found in hospitality opens a space for the presence of the other in kindness and generosity. We are hospitable to the stranger and guest. Hospitality views the other, not as an interloper, but as an opportunity to tangibly manifest our relationship with God. We offer a free and fearless space for the tired traveler on the journey. This space must be consciously held clear of our own demands and expectations, foregoing any agenda that uses the other for our own purposes.

Whenever company comes to the Powers' house, a big pot of pinto beans bubbles on the stove. Cook some cornbread, slice a few tomatoes and dinner is on. Maybe the missionaries visiting from India need a place to perch. Or the friend in town on business wants a break from one more sterile hotel room.

Give someone a clean bed, fresh towels and a decent meal ... you never know how long they will stay. If the beans are bubbling when Joni's family comes home, they likely as not ask, "So who's staying tonight?"

> Let mutual love continue. Do not neglect to show hospitality to strangers, for by doing that some have entertained angels without knowing it. Remember those who are in prison, as though you were in prison with them; those who are being tortured, as though you yourselves were being tortured. Hebrews 13

 We must be intentional in the purpose, timing and extent of sacrificial love. The Son came in the fullness of time to redeem humanity unto God for the distinct and sole purpose of God's glory. Human whim and desire do not hold us in their clutch, to be whipped about to and fro. We serve God alone as we love others for God's sake and will answer to God alone for the choices we make. God does not call us to spend ourselves unwisely for personal pride or out of neglectful passivity. Just because you are able does not necessarily mean you are called.

We love Paul's short account of Apollos, an early church member. "Now concerning our brother Apollos. I strongly urged him to visit you with the other brothers, but he was not at all willing to come now. He will come when he has the opportunity." We wonder how that conversation between the two of them went. Paul had a forceful personality that held nothing back. No telling what "strongly urged" meant! But Apollos stood firm for whatever reason he had in not coming. Paul seemed resigned to the outcome, noting that Apollos would come when he had the opportunity. Have you said no to anything lately?

By my rules, caring for troubled people always
took preference over enjoying delightful people,
and the line of troubled people never ended...
I wondered why I had not changed that rule sooner.

Barbara Brown Taylor

 Loving well requires both a giving up and a putting
on. In Colossians 3, Paul called the people out of
bitterness and wrath. Simultaneously, he command-
ed them to clothe themselves in humility and kindness. The question is not only "Do you have enemies?" but goes
further to "Are you dying for your enemies, friends, family and
strangers?" It is an active love enveloping more than a lack of
rancor. Do you gather up your entire being and offer it with
open palms to the world? Are the first fruits of your time and
resources—not the dregs and leftovers—at God's disposal?

Just before the officials arrested Jesus, he and the disciples
were visiting a home in Bethany. A woman came and began
pouring precious perfume over Jesus' head. The disciples could
not believe she wasted such a priceless asset, arguing that she
should have sold it to feed the poor. Jesus said the woman had
done a good deed in preparing him for burial. Her gesture
showed extravagant love for the Lord. She *poured* the perfume
on his head instead of dabbing a little behind his ears.

But who am I, and what is my people, that we should be
able to make this freewill offering? For all things come
from you, and of your own have we given you. For we
are aliens and transients before you, as were all our an-
cestors; our days on the earth are like a shadow, and
there is no hope. O LORD our God, all this abundance
that we have provided for building you a house for your
holy name comes from your hand and is all your own.

1 Chronicles 29

Setting aside the priority or "firstness" of self requires sacrifice. You do not jockey for position, but gladly step aside as another moves to the front of the line. Waving the rulebook in people's faces may be your way of protecting your rights. If everyone plays by the rules, you have a fair chance of winning the game. Putting your life at God's disposal means you do not own a rulebook. God's ways will not be your ways. Your reputation ceases to be the point as you seek to reflect God's reputation. You who reveled in the letter of the law abandon that pursuit for the greater good of loving others well.

John the Baptist wandered the countryside in a garment of camel's hair, eating locust and honey. "Repent: for the kingdom of heaven is at hand!" People thronged to see him. He baptized many of them in the Jordan River, while calling the religious leaders a "brood of vipers" to their faces. But when the people began to wonder whether John the Baptist might be the Messiah, he quickly turned those rumors aside: "He who is mightier than I is coming, and I am not fit to untie the thong of His sandals." Jesus sought the prophet out and asked to be baptized by him. What an unfathomable privilege for the man in the camel hair cloak.

> Such is the confidence that we have through Christ toward God. Not that we are competent of ourselves to claim anything as coming from us; our competence is from God, who has made us competent to be ministers of a new covenant, not of letter but of spirit; for the letter kills, but the Spirit gives life. 2 Corinthians 3

An odd trend has surfaced in many churches. Gift surveys attempt to identify which spiritual gifts God has bestowed upon you. Someone grades the survey, and you then become the proud owner of your special gift such as exhortation or administration.

This frighteningly efficient approach concerns us because people quickly begin to worship the gift over the Giver. They narrow their service to those opportunities that supposedly optimize their effectiveness. Christ calls us to lay down the whole of our lives. We are generalists in love, not specialists.

Our friend Sashi is a brilliant heart surgeon with years of experience. When he volunteers with a disability ministry, you might expect he would do surgery. However Sashi travels to developing countries to deliver and fit wheelchairs. You can find him in a small village in Cuba, wandering among a shipment of refurbished chairs, looking for the perfect headrest to modify for a young man's enlarged, misshapen head. Hours later, the family wheels their son out into the sunshine for the first time in his life. Sashi's makeshift contraption of plywood, duct tape, foam and lots of love works perfectly.

I appeal to you therefore, brothers and sisters, by the mercies of God, to present your bodies as a living sacrifice, holy and acceptable to God, which is your spiritual worship. Let love be genuine. Contribute to the needs of saints. Extend hospitality to strangers. Live peaceably with all. Romans 12

 Community plays an important role in both cultivating and teaching sacrificial love. You learn by being loved well and by watching others love well. The learning flows through generations and neighborhoods and church congregations. You sacrifice for me, and I in turn sacrifice for another in an unbroken circle of caring. Love can be imitated and replicated powerfully. The expressions of sacrifice gather momentum like individual streams running downhill, converging into the rushing waters of a river.

What I Learned from My Mother
by Julia Kasdorf

I learned from my mother how to love
the living, to have plenty of vases on hand
in case you have to rush to the hospital
with peonies cut from the lawn, black ants
still stuck to the buds. I learned to save jars
large enough to hold fruit salad for a whole
grieving household, to cube home-canned pears
and peaches, to slice through maroon grape skins
and flick out the sexual seeds with a knife point.
I learned to attend viewings even if I didn't know
the deceased, to press the moist hands
of the living, to look in their eyes and offer
sympathy, as though I understood loss even then.
I learned that whatever we say means nothing,
what anyone will remember is that we came.
I learned to believe I had the power to ease
awful pains materially like an angel.
Like a doctor, I learned to create
from another's suffering my own usefulness, and once
you know how to do this, you can never refuse.
To every house you enter, you must offer
healing: a chocolate cake you baked yourself,
the blessing of your voice, your chaste touch.

In "Gift," we discuss how the process of forgiveness requires a willingness to let the Spirit move. Likewise, you learn sacrificial love by giving the Spirit access to your life. Even if you are miserly, clinging and closed, guarding your mattress stuffed with treasures, there is hope. Even if you outwardly demonstrate constant sacrifice but inwardly seethe with resentment or pride, there is hope. Even if you have sacrificed for years, caring for your wife after her stroke and are now spent and exhausted from the effort, there is hope. The Spirit can and will transform your affection for life at God's disposal. The Redeemer of Life joyfully leads the way in sacrificial love.

Chances are you sang a song about the tax-collector Zaccheus if you were in church as a young child. "Zaccheus was a wee little man; a wee little man was he." He was a rich man and short. Zaccheus wanted to see who this Jesus was, so he climbed a sycamore tree to get a better view over the passing crowd. Jesus spied him up in the tree and called, "Zaccheus, hurry and come down, for today I must stay at your house." Zaccheus not only hosted Jesus but declared he would give half his possessions to the poor. Talk about a willingness to let the Spirit move!

Therefore my heart is glad, and my soul rejoices; my body also rests secure. For you do not give me up to Sheol, or let your faithful one see the Pit. You show me the path of life. In your presence there is fullness of joy; in your right hand are pleasures forevermore. Psalm 16

• • • • • stop a moment

Glance back through the signposts. Which thoughts are new for you? We used examples like Joni's pot of beans and Zaccheus' dramatic turn. Did personal examples come to mind as you read? Where have you found the greatest joy in sacrifice? Which signpost needs the most prayer in your life right now?

●　　●　　●　　●　　●

Someday you may literally save another's life by substituting your own. You may take a bullet or shield someone from harm. There are thousands of stories of this kind of sacrifice in war, in natural disasters and in other moments of crisis. Most people hope they would make this sacrifice if ever given the chance. Some of you already know the answer to that choice. Few of us will ever find out.

More often, you pour life into others by serving them. You put your time and resources at their disposal. You cry when they cry and laugh when they laugh. You listen to stories that change you in the hearing. You cannot stand off from the experience of loving because in it you find God. You put your life in front of people as an encouragement, not in its perfection, but in its pursuit of your fully human purpose. Your presence brings hope, which is the topic of our next chapter, "Sight."

What does sacrifice look like for you today and tomorrow? Walking away from the next job promotion because it would put your family on the sacrificial altar? Taking care of the widows and orphans and poor and downtrodden who have no resources and no standing in the eyes of this world? Helping your elderly father get to the sixth floor doctor's office after his eyes and legs fail him? Not snapping at that same elderly father when he asks "What did you say?" for the hundredth time? Showing up when a friend calls from the middle of some hell? Or offering your home to that missionary family when it would be so much easier just to put a little money in the offering plate?

Sacrifice is the unmerited, undeserved favor of our lives laid down for the sake of God . . . with gladness. Perhaps we have not taken a bullet for anyone, but we give ourselves away, five minutes at a time, one commitment at a time, for the rest of our lives. Blood, sweat and tears pave the way. Joy beyond measure awaits us.

"Ascribe to the LORD the glory due his name; bring an offering, and come into his courts."

What's lost

is nothing to what's found,

and all the death

that ever was,

set next to life,

would scarcely fill a cup.

Frederick Buechner

LifeSpace™

chapter eleven

SIG

HT

Almost 50,000 words have passed before your eyes thus far in this book. We have poured out our passion: crafting sentences, arranging paragraphs and designing pages to deliver the message. Only if this chapter is true does any of that effort matter. We turn to hope as the litmus test for what is real about this life with God.

As we state in the beginning, a fully human life is an existence that reflects the knowledge of God and trust in God through an expansive experience of living. With God as the expansive center of life, the size of your hope depends on the size of your God. Big vision, big God. Small vision, then despair stands right around the corner.

Life expands when the future holds promise. We breathe without hesitation. We look forward with expectation, confident of a positive outcome. The Creator God, as sovereign over time and space, promises life eternal for those who believe the gospel of Christ. That life cannot be fearful and cautious as if the future holds a fierce unknown. God promises life over death, abundance over scarcity and joy over sorrow. Amid clouds of dust, we must train our eyes to catch the shards of Light that are harbingers of heaven.

source of hope

Our Father which art in heaven,
Hallowed be thy name.
Thy kingdom come.
Thy will be done in earth,
as it is in heaven.

The Lord's Prayer rolls off many of our tongues. It identifies God as the source of hope: "Our Father which art in heaven ..." It anticipates the kingdom as the content of hope: "... in earth, as it is in heaven." The passage is rightly ordered because you cannot talk about what you hope *for* until you take a hard look at what you hope *in*.

We have confidence in the God of covenant love. We trust the person of God to be faithful, steadfast, sufficient and gracious in love toward us. Lesser loves of power and might—a king with a great army or a muscled war horse—are futile. Our faith rests on a persistent belief or settled conviction that God will single-handedly bring to pass divine promises.

The LORD looks down from heaven;
    he sees all humankind.
From where he sits enthroned he watches
    all the inhabitants of the earth—
he who fashions the hearts of them all,
    and observes their deeds.
A king is not saved by his great army;
    a warrior is not delivered by his great strength.
The war horse is vain hope for victory,
    and by its great might it cannot save.
Truly the eye of the LORD is on those who fear him,
    on those who hope in his steadfast love,
to deliver their soul from death,
    and to keep them alive in famine.
Our soul waits for the LORD;
    he is our help and shield.
Our heart is glad in him,
    because we trust in his holy name. Psalm 33

What has God promised? An answer of territory or comfort or prosperity reveals a limited and self-indulgent vision. We speak against several popular conceptions of God as promise-maker. There is no little book of promises that we can keep on our dashboard to check off as God comes through for us. Health, check. Wealth, check. Peace, check. A nice mother-in-law, check. Obedient kids, check. A successful church building campaign, check. Scripture provides no such list, and the presumption of a book on our dashboard borders on blasphemy. God has promised God. God has promised life. The specific complexion of fulfillment remains in God's hands.

Similarly, God is not a vending machine or Santa Claus holding your Christmas list of "I wants." You cannot coerce circumstances or outcomes by manipulating God. Maybe you try praying a particular prayer three times while standing on your head or turning your baseball cap counterclockwise or never eating black jelly beans.

We hedge our bets with these attempts to influence the luck of cosmic alignment. We deny God as personal and powerful in such contortions of pride. Our actions or lack thereof will not thwart the purposes of God. We are called to a persistent hope in what God can and will deliver.

· · · · · **stop a moment**

The flannel graph used to be a favorite tool for teachers before this computer age. A large square board was covered with felt. Objects and characters also made of felt were stuck to the board as the teacher told a story or taught a concept. The child chosen as the flannel graph assistant enjoyed the height of privilege.

If someone asked you to present a flannel graph of your dream for life, what pieces would you put on it? Would there be certain kinds of people such as a spouse or child? Would you put any objects like a house on it? How would your career appear? How would you depict your dream for life with God? Stop to think about the picture and jot the elements in the frame.

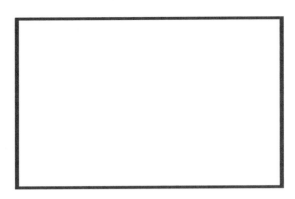

We often limit hope to the flannel graph. We build a picture of the perfect life and pin our hopes on all the pieces falling into place. Surely it is our right to expect a particular picture to come true. Time passes. The vibrant felt colors fade. Pieces fall off as life's disappointments arise. Your dream spouse never arrives. Ill health plagues you. A business fails. Ministry burns you out. Eventually the board becomes quite bare—a skeleton of the original dream. Apathy sets in and we stop believing God works on our behalf.

• • • • •

God has not promised to fit onto our flannel graph. Living hope means that for every dream that falls by the wayside, a richer dream takes its place. The discipline of hope embraces an ever-changing kaleidoscope of possibility. There is so much more, and we have no idea what we are missing.

The lesser hopes of this world
result in minimalist dreams.

Expand your sights on hope. God goes for the gusto. How about life instead of death? Incomprehensible, never-cresting joy? Peace beyond measure? Nostrils full of holy air? Can you really manufacture hope that beats any of that?

God promises eternal life for those who believe in Jesus Christ: "Truly, truly, I say to you, he who hears My word, and believes Him who sent Me, has eternal life, and does not come into judgment, but has passed out of death into life." This promise begins in the now—*has* eternal life, *has* passed out of death—and continues for eternity.

God promises resurrected life in which real transformation occurs. The promises straddle dimensions of time. In the words of the apostle Peter, we have "an inheritance which is imperishable and undefiled and will not fade away, reserved in heaven for you." God promises to be our "very present help in time of trouble." Future resurrection combined with present sustenance brings unshakeable hope. Jürgen Moltmann wrote of the self-emptying response that should result from the promises of God:

> The resurrection hope makes people ready to live their lives in love wholly, and to say a full and entire Yes to a life that leads to death. It does not withdraw the human soul from bodily, sensory life; it ensouls this life with unending joy. In expectation of the resurrection of the dead, the person who hopes casts away the soul's protective cloak in which the wounded heart has wrapped itself.

complexion of hope

E. F. Harrison, a New Testament scholar, calls hope "expectation yoked with confidence and desire." In Paul's words, we "groan inwardly while we wait for adoption, for the redemption of our bodies. For in hope we were saved. Now hope that is seen is not hope. For who hopes for what is seen? But if we hope for what we do not see, we wait for it with patience." By faith in the gospel of Christ, we expect transformation by the Spirit of

God, confident that God will bring this desired end to fruition. Hope gives faith its wings.

John 9 tells of Jesus encountering a blind man alongside the road. Jesus spit in the dirt and smeared the mud on the sightless eyes. He then instructed the man to go wash in a particular pool. Still without sight, the man demonstrated faith by going to the pool, and his sight was restored. The man was questioned several times afterward about the incident (as you can imagine!). He answered consistently that he had been blind, Jesus worked a miracle, and now he could see.

Jesus used the miracle of the blind man as a metaphor for sight that goes beyond the present circumstances. God graciously expands our vision to encompass the greater reality of the kingdom. What begins now will be completed when we gaze on Christ's face. "For now we see in a mirror, dimly, but then we will see face to face. Now I know only in part; then I will know fully, even as I have been fully known." In the present, daggers of Light shoot across our field of vision for brief glimpses of glory that speak of promise.

Although you have not seen him, you love him; and even though you do not see him now, you believe in him and rejoice with an indescribable and glorious joy, for you are receiving the outcome of your faith, the salvation of your souls. Through him you have come to trust in God, who raised him from the dead and gave him glory, so that your faith and hope are set on God. 1 Peter 1

We yearn for God's glory to shine brightly throughout the universe, for the restoration of creation to be complete, for human history to be redeemed in our fully human purpose and for humanity to join Christ in resurrected life. As we wait, often with great impatience, Christ goes ahead of us as representative of what will be.

In Christ, we see the very future of humanity. According to Hebrews 6, "We have this hope, a sure and steadfast anchor of the soul, a hope that enters the inner shrine behind the curtain, where Jesus, a forerunner on our behalf, has entered, having become a high priest forever." The paradox remains: we see and do not see behind the curtain now.

Sometimes we balance precariously on the fence of hope. Fall off one side into despair. Fall off the other into presumption. Despair assumes you know what God will not do. It is the sin of abandoned possibility. The old English language used the word "wanhope" for hope that has waned into despair. Hear Maya Angelou's words, excerpted from her poem, "A Plagued Journey," about the deathly nature of wanhope:

> Through all the bright hours
> I cling to expectations, until
> darkness comes to reclaim me
> as its own. Hope fades, day is gone
> into its irredeemable place
> and I am thrown back into the familiar
> bonds of disconsolation.
> Gloom crawls around
> lapping lasciviously
> between my toes, at my ankles,
> and it sucks the strands of my
> hair. It forgives my heady
> fling with Hope. I am
> joined again into its
> greedy arms.

While despair assumes God will not act, presumption assumes God will. We sin by manufacturing possibility apart from the promises of God. It is as if you see your colleague with a gift card to the local coffee shop, so you magnanimously invite the office out for lattes. Your colleague had no idea she was hosting a party. It is not your gift card, but you presume upon it. Hope strikes a delicate balance. You can only say, "I will ask and then wait upon the Lord." You cannot wrestle God to the mat or box God in with an incomplete or incorrect vision for all that can and will be.

• • • • • a story from Bob

For many years I taught a class for young couples at our church. Most had recently married and brimmed full of hope. They dreamed of homes, children, careers and long life together. As I listened to their plans, my response most often was an injection of what I called realism. "You are going to get pregnant next August so you can have the baby in May? Hmmm. Have you considered the possibility that things might not go exactly as planned?"

Eventually life experience tempered their enthusiastic hopefulness. Struggles with infertility, money, marriage, family and other issues dampened the couples' dreams. Some situations passed into despair. I remember a conversation with a father whose two young children were severely disabled. "What do you hope for?" I asked. From the way he looked at me, I might as well have been speaking a foreign language. After a long pause, he said softly, "I guess I don't much hope."

We have a skewed understanding of realism. To us, being realistic means expecting closed doors. Realism can be about resignation and cynicism. It has more than a hint of endurance by gutting life out. We start out hopeful and then go downhill from that instant forward. The more we know, the less we hope. What if the most hopeful I will ever be was as a child with a quarter in my pocket and a ride to the candy store?

It is both a gift and a discipline for hope to expand over time. Expansive life with God means the more I know and experience, the more I hope. I have to re-text realism to wrap around God as the Really Real. Potential and possibility exist with God. I cannot be an ostrich with my head in the sand, denying the data in front of me. Instead, my eyes are fully open, recognizing the reality I can see, and searching for the reality beyond me. I need kingdom eyes of quixotic wonder.

What do I hope for at this juncture of life? I hope for the Spirit's gift of hopefulness. I hope that I will see and take delight in the glory of God. I hope that transformation happens as my affection embraces true loveliness. I hope for the benevolent face of God toward me and those I love—not because I think it is promised, but because it is grace and I yearn for it. I hope I will love others well. I hope for rest or at least for endurance to persevere without it. I hope for God to be glorified in all that I am as a human being. I hope that God lets me see that my life matters for the purpose of God's glory.

For me, hope feels like pushing against all the imperfections of this present while appreciating the moments that sometimes come remarkably close to being perfect. I watch as I wait because I want to see.

● ● ● ● ●

imperative of hope

Life over death brings . . .
Assurance of presence
Peace for eternity
Delight in God
Rest in love

Too often Christian hope sees an apocalyptic, final solution to the ills of this world. Stroll through your neighborhood bookstore and look at all the titles about the end times.

Perhaps your pastor has shown some amazing schematics describing Armageddon, the beast and other fantastical prophecies. Here is what we know: God's kingdom has been inaugurated with Christ and will be fully realized in eternity. How we get from here to there can be hotly debated. Whatever happens, we highly recommend seat belts because things will likely get a little wild.

We must not be a people in waiting, holding our breath until this earthy offense to our senses ends and real life with God begins. We should not wear hazardous waste suits to shield us from the present facts. God breathed life into us for the purpose of reflecting God's glory and delighting in God. The psalmist asked, "Where would I be if I did not believe I would experience the LORD's favor in the land of the living?" Seize the moment now without holding back. As Moltmann writes:

> The notion that this life is no more than a preparation for a life beyond is the theory of a refusal to live, and a religious fraud. It is inconsistent with the living God, who is a "lover of life." In that sense, it is religious atheism.... But human life is livingness, and human livingness means to be interested, to be concerned. Concern in life is what we call love. True human life comes from love, is alive in love, and through loving makes something living of other life too.

Hope moves from the individual to the community to creation in ever outward spheres of concern. Hoping for the kingdom of God to be realized does not allow for an incurved, singular view. The author of Hebrews 10 specifically tied our confession of hope to our concern for others:

> Let us draw near with a sincere heart in full assurance of faith, having our hearts sprinkled clean from an evil

conscience and our bodies washed with pure water. Let us hold fast the confession of our hope without wavering, for He who promised is faithful; and let us consider how to stimulate one another to love and good deeds, not forsaking our own assembling together, as is the habit of some, but encouraging one another; and all the more, as you see the day drawing near.

We must not hunker down in the basement with our bottles of water and dehydrated food to wait for Christ to beam us up to heaven. Nor should we dance, solitary and stripped bare, on a mountaintop. As we see the day drawing near, we stimulate one another to love, assemble together and encourage one another. With full assurance of our fate, we should be absolutely dangerous in love since we have nothing to lose!

Being a person of hope does not mean you deny the real needs of people for a Pollyanna-ish view of transcendent life. A starving woman hopes for a sandwich. Love that person by giving her a sandwich. Be Christ to her and let grace lift her gaze toward God.

tension of hope

Hope works on several levels. The spiritual songs sung by slaves often held double meaning. The lyrics obviously revealed a yearning for heaven. Underneath, a nuanced meaning sought relief from the cruelty of their slavery. Hope is both immediate and distant. By loving others well, we wrap incarnation around hope and let it soar. Angelou spoke of incarnated hope in another of her poems:

The horizon leans forward,
Offering you space
To place new steps of change …
Here, on the pulse of this new day,
You may have the grace to look up and out
And into your sister's eyes,
And into your brother's face,
Your country,
And say simply
Very simply
With hope—
Good morning.

We must straddle a tension until the day we stand with Christ in the throne room of God. We are a people of two worlds. With Christ as the bridge, we stand with one foot on earth and one foot in heaven. Reminds us of a U.S. monument called Four Corners. You can stand **we** there and be in New Mexico, Colorado, should be Utah and Arizona at the same time. Children absolutely play hopscotch, jumping from one state dangerous to another. in love

Our straddle of dual citizenship means delight will necessarily be interwoven with yearning. Our best days here should simultaneously bring a praise of thanksgiving and a prayer for a more perfect day to come. The disciples of Jesus kept their eyes open for the return of the Messiah. He promised to come back. How long, O Lord, must we wait?

· · · · · a story from Joni

We have a place in Colorado alongside a mountain river, sheltered by a stand of aspen trees under an ice blue sky. A fallen tree lies there beside the water. When Providence aligns all my stars

in a grand stroke of blessing, I am sitting on that log, and Beauty visits me.

I lie back and let Beauty wash over me. The clouds march through the sky, going somewhere or nowhere. My hands lift with fingers spread as I watch the dance of the silver dollar aspen leaves in the sunlight. The roar of rapids twirls around in my head. Voices from the many pasts of being in this place keep up a muffled chorus in the background—my grandparents, my parents and now my children. Their ghosts twitter in and out of my memory. My spirit dances with joy like a wood fairy. I begin to melt into this place.

Predictably, the delight soon interlaces with something else. It feels like an ache inside a joint that cannot be relieved with the touch of massaging hands. The ache is a shadow that Beauty brings, attached inextricably to the pleasure. I sense one cannot exist without the other.

Beauty seems to carry the ache with her. I feel it in a saxophone's run up the scale of a smoky jazz piece and when my daughter sashays out in her new Easter outfit. The ache encompasses me while dancing in Peru, spinning around a grand balcony, wearing a long dress of gossamer green silk. I ache as I stand in the museum in Spain, enthralled by resplendent paintings of Christ. Beauty bursts forth with such joy. Beauty lingers with such ache.

Beauty aches with limit. Creation groans in yearning for someone or something that once was and will yet someday be. It yearns for the sacred romance of God with creation. Whispers of lost glory wait to be regained. The ache comes from standing in the presence of the Divine and knowing I have but a taste of the entire possibility.

Beauty aches with being. Much like God told Moses in the Old Testament, "I Am who I Am," Beauty simply is. I can never own Beauty. While my family may own the place in Colorado, creation owns Beauty. While I can possess objects of Beauty, I cannot

possess her power. The ache comes from grasping too tightly.
A closed fist cannot hold Beauty.

Beauty aches with time. I know the hours and days move
without me. They do not sit still. Eternity calls. The ache comes
from wanting to stop time and to freeze the frame of Beauty.
Freeze the river currents. But suspending time would change the
nature of Beauty. The saxophone's song would not be the same if
one note played endlessly. The song must move. Eternity lurks
just beyond my reach. So close and yet so far.

Beauty aches with grace. While in this tent, mortality burdens
us. Beauty is the deposit for a future lightness of being. Her grace
lessens the gravity of this time. She serves as a marker for the past
memory, the present moment and the future hope—all at once.
The common thread is the touch of grace, the undeserved favor.
The transition from gravity to grace and from heaviness to light-
ness brings an ache.

The veil between this reality and the next flutters softly to and
fro, allowing glimpses of heaven's light. The blaze of joy blends
seamlessly with the lurking shadows. Beauty stands at the cur-
tain, pulling my eyes toward the shining glory on the other side.
It is all I can do to stay here. Those silver dollar leaves and that
chorus of voices gently tether me.

There is a place in Colorado. When Providence aligns all
my stars in a grand stroke of blessing, I am sitting by a river.
Beauty visits me.

●　　●　　●　　●　　●

Gregory of Nyssa, an early church theologian, understood the
portal of Beauty into the heart of God. He wrote of a desire for a
headlong journey toward God, fueled by the beautiful:

And the true vision of God consists in this, in never
reaching satiety of the desire. We ought always to look
through the things that we can see and still be on fire

with the desire to see more. So let there be no limit to curtail our growth in our journey upwards to God. This is because no limit to the beautiful has been found nor can any satiety cut short the progress of the soul in its desire for the beautiful.

We are of this world and alien to it. Christ represents us in heaven yet we are not there. Where we are, Christ once was. Where Christ is, we will someday be. Christ allows us a view into God's glory that our eyes do not see clearly. You cannot say that this earthly life represents one reality and then heavenly life another. God burst into our world in the incarnation and blurred the line between now and later, here and there. Eternity takes up our temporal time. The kingdom of God is already and not yet. That horizon provides a broad space for mystery, possibility and hope.

> Possibility in hope means . . .
> Transformation happens
> Circumstances change
> Horizons appear
> Love prevails

We often limit hope to the absence of the negative. This perspective denies the presence of the positive. Life abundant will prevail. Revelation 21 describes the new heaven and new earth of God's realized kingdom. It does celebrate the absence of sin's sorrow: "See, the home of God is among mortals. He will dwell with them; they will be his peoples, and God himself will be with them; he will wipe every tear from their eyes. Death will be no more; mourning and crying and pain will be no more." But the description goes on to extol the making of all things new:

Then the angel showed me the river of the water of life, bright as crystal, flowing from the throne of God and of the Lamb through the middle of the street of the city. And there will be no more night; they need no light of lamp or sun, for the Lord God will be their light, and they will reign forever and ever.

Remember the box and the expanding sphere we describe in the first chapter? The box represents our efforts to contain and control this life with God as we put masking tape lines on the floor. Hope has to be more than folding up those boxes and putting them in a storage closet in case we need them later. True hope grabs that sphere as it expands into eternity and holds on for the ride.

The lesser hopes to which we cling—like safety, equity, prosperity or stability—give false comfort. Hope in God requires that we admit two things: first, that God controls the content, process, means and timing of our lives; and second, that we live with human limitations of embodiment and finitude.

True hope can be as humbling as it is liberating.

We must acknowledge the daily deaths of this present life, large and small. Minimizing the very real presence of death does a profane disservice to life. We experience the inconsolable grief of loss this side of heaven, and those who traffic in joy know it intimately. Christ bids us to follow him through the sorrow of the cross to resurrection. No shortcuts allowed.

So how does hope happen? As we write in the chapter on "Breath," the Spirit of God produces hope in us: "May the God of hope fill you with all joy and peace in believing, so that you may abound in hope by the power of the Holy Spirit." The Spirit opens your eyes to see and your ears to hear. Once again, you do not muster a particular attitude. The Spirit marries the knowledge of God and trust in God to lift your gaze and expand your view.

With unveiled faces, seeing the glory of the Lord, we are being transformed. Indifference ignites into passion. Rebellion loses its allure. The boxes disappear. The sphere expands. Life moves from shades of gray to the colors of the rainbow. Our eyes watch for possibility on the horizon. Shards of Light shoot across our field of vision. Hope is born and nurtured like stars in the nurseries of heavenly galaxies.

Other people lift our gaze as they bring testimony of God's work in their lives. They provide a collective memory of and witness to the Spirit's transforming power. When we despair, people move to be hope for us. They shield us from the storm, listen to our ranting and remind us of our faith. They incubate hope until it burns brightly once more in us.

The Word of God spurs us to hope by revealing the person of God. The narrative passages record God's purpose in creation and faithfulness to humanity. The Psalms use poetry and song to praise God for deliverance and help in time of trouble. The prophets show God's grace in mercy. And the gospels bring us the good news of Jesus Christ and eternal life. Revelation closes with a picture of the river of life streaming down the streets of heaven.

Hope may begin as a faint ember under a pile of ashes, hardly visible to the naked eye. Through the Spirit, other human beings and the Word, God stokes the fire. God's purposes will prevail. The kingdom will come. Without a doubt, the mystery is great. May hope abound to the glory of God.

> Our Father which art in heaven,
> Hallowed be thy name.
> Thy kingdom come.
> Thy will be done in earth,
> as it is in heaven.

God Speaks in Blue
Luci Shaw

My friend hands me a gift

from overseas. "Here," she says.

"For you." The small packet rustles

with dry particles; through thin paper

my fingers feel the nubs. I thank her,

turning over the plain brown envelope.

There, from the other side, a photo—

the vivid, blunt cross of *Mecanopsis Betonicifolia*,

a Himalayan Blue Poppy—looks at me with

its gold eye, four azure petals blazing.

A blue to color a dream. The blue

of Mary's mantle according to Raphael.

The blue at the heart of a gas flame, within

an ice cave, on a cerulean door in a white wall

on Santorini, a kind of blue that

catches my heart ajar and blows it wide open.

Dry seeds and a picture, until next spring.

But, oh, if only I could be alive enough

to burn like this flower. If only

I could bloom as blue as this.

chapter twelve

The practice

of life with God

The instructor turns up the heat as she enters the room. Muscles will slowly become supple and lithe in the warmth. People straggle in: some chatting amicably, others solitary with the weight of the day on their shoulders. New students choose borrowed mats of bright blue or sunny yellow. Their faces bear countenance of either hope or anxiety about the next hour. These folks are gently directed to open spaces on the floor, allowing plenty of room for leg spans and arm reaches.

The yoga class begins with an entreaty from the instructor: "Please dedicate your practice today to a purpose of your choosing. Perhaps to healing or maybe to joy. You might practice as a prayer to your Higher Power. Be intentional. Practice generosity as you look upon the faces of the people around you. We come together in this room in order not to be alone. Be patient with yourself, as the practice of yoga never finishes, but only changes."

Inhale, hold. Exhale, hold. The breath warms the body with its energy. The first poses come easily. Class veterans close their eyes and move smoothly through the sequences. New practitioners closely watch the front of the room as they attempt to mimic the movements. The poses progress in difficulty, challenging balance and strength. Everyone crashes out of a pose here and there. The instructor encourages boldness. Falling on your head is grounds for a quiet celebration of courage. "Don't forget to breathe," she says.

The bodies run the spectrum of diversity: short, tall, large, small, female, male, young, old, light, dark, straight, bent. Some strike the poses with serene faces, gazing at the ceiling with calm and ease. Others grimace and groan, hold their breath and generally flop their way through the class. All come voluntarily.

The communal practice is the point.

The favorite pose finally arrives at the end of class. Everyone lies flat on their backs, eyes closed, limbs limp. The reward of rest is cherished. The instructor calls the students to closure with, "Thank you for practicing together today. Blessings upon you."

The practice of life with God is like yoga class with a goal of practicing well together. We do not embrace a mantra of "Practice makes perfect." Each person brings a different perspective, a different story, a different center of gravity. Space is made for all. Some days your life moves in concert with others as the love of God shines through you. Other days the best you can do is show up and try not to take out the person next to you.

We write this book for all who need to breathe. We write for all who want to experience anew the life-giving breath of the Creator. The sum of our words condenses into the scripture from John: "For God so loved the world, that he gave his only begotten Son, that whosoever believeth in him should not perish but have everlasting life." Nothing in those words is small or suffocating or constricting or narrowing or boxy. It is the good news—the gospel—that brings an expansive experience of living with the holy God of this universe.

Through Christ, we enjoy access to the triune God. Freedom reigns as God's kingdom comes. Death is vanquished and life prevails. You can breathe. If this book has done nothing else, we pray it has given you the space to be fully human: LifeSpace.

This is the *practice* of life with God.
It never finishes
but only changes.

Throughout our writing, we acknowledge this life with God as both gift and discipline. Obedience to the law of love requires the gift of transformation by the Spirit and our willingness to engage in the process of change. The classic spiritual disciplines are well used by the Spirit to change the affection of the heart. Meditation, prayer, fasting, study, solitude, service, confession, silence, simplicity, chastity and other practices place us in a stance of readiness for God's presence.

We embrace these disciplines with the caution that their purpose must serve God's purpose. They do not earn our salvation or God's ongoing favor. They are not the subject of life with God. The disciplines help us lay ourselves in the way of allurement.

We believe much broader disciplines are also important to our practice. The discipline of delight means you acknowledge and celebrate the glorious person of God. Kingdom eyes seek to see God at work in this world. The discipline requires that you actively forsake indifference, rebellion or performance in order to pursue expansive life. Patient perseverance rests in the promises of God.

As with the yoga class, the practice of life with God works as a communal endeavor. We join together as fellow pilgrims on a journey. Accordingly, the discipline of loving others well honors the unique calling of humanity in each and every face you see. You lavish grace as you lollygag with and show up for others. You forgive unceasingly, seek forgiveness easily and sacrifice with gladness. You embody hope for people burdened with despair. You fling yourself upon the world in confession of a God whose love endures forever.

The sacrament of communion, practiced by the church since the time of Christ, expresses hope well. We remember the history of Christ's death, look forward to his coming and trust him to sustain us with the bread and wine of life in the present. The ritual preserves our collective memory of the gospel. It communicates our story to the next generation. We share the grace of God as we commune with others around the table.

The concepts of LifeSpace are not novel but ancient. For an eternity, life has and will center on God as Creator of all. This truth beckons humanity back from box-building forays, where God has been relegated to the sidelines as the self steps forward. It calls us out of self-absorbed indifference and shortsighted rebellion. With this writing, we resoundingly lift our voices in exalted praise of the Really Real in the practice of being fully human.

We invite you to join in the ongoing conversation around LifeSpace. This book acts as a field guide of sorts, and you are a reporter in the field. We want to know where you see God and how the Holy Spirit moves.

As we say in the beginning, the best situation would be one in which we are all in the same room or on the same hiking trail. We could see you and get to know you. In the meantime, let us hear from you. A conversation has already begun, and we would love for you to jump in with both feet! We want to encourage you as we learn from you.

We pray that you will actively practice what you have learned in these pages. Pay attention to what you read and hear. Notice an exalted love of self in much of the popular media and in the sermons coming from many pulpits, for that matter. Use this book as a stimulus for your own exploration of how expansive life can be. The truth of God should affect your next breath. Has it? Does it? Will it? You must be bold. Forget about thinking outside the box. Forget about a box all together. We like these words from an insurance advertisement:

> Life is a tornado watch.
> You can hunker down in the basement,
> or get up on the roof,
> let the wind give you rock star hair
> and yell,
> I knew you were coming.
> That's why I didn't rake the leaves.

Lay down your fears. Grab your mat. Find a free space and start to move. Breathe deeply. Choose Life as you fling love. May all glory abound to the Holy One.

The LifeSpace Prayer

Gracious God, we stand in awe of you.
You reign over the heavens
and the earth without peer.
You created humanity to reflect
the beams of your shining glory.
Turn our gaze toward your loveliness
and your perfection.
May our delight find no end in you, our first love.

As sinners, we pursue lesser loves
and are too easily satisfied.
We acknowledge that you alone
provided for our redemption through your Son.
The provision is fully sufficient
and can be neither diminished
nor supplemented.
We celebrate Christ's victory
over the power of death for eternity.
Christ ever remains our living Savior,
our Mediator and our High Priest.

Thank you, God, for sending the Holy Spirit
as your agent of change.
In the Spirit we draw our life's breath.
Fix our affection on the beauty of your holiness.
May the Spirit's transforming power woo us
toward love for you.

Encourage us to live expansively as we abandon
suffocating self-interest.

We desire to love as you have loved us, God.
Move us to lay ourselves down
as sacrificial life-givers.
Enable us to forgive just as you forgive us.
We beg to see your grace flow over us
and from us like a refreshing river.
Spur us to love each other well for your sake.

You are our one Great Hope, God.
We grasp at a poverty of other hopes
inadequate for the struggles of this world.
Remind us of your promises for abundant life
and your eternal presence with us.
Ground our hope in your sovereignty,
your goodness and your faithfulness.
Bring freedom and liberation
through the resurrection power of Christ.

We lift our words as an offering of praise
and thanksgiving to you, God.
You alone deserve glory and honor
above all creation.
O Lord God, we yearn to see your face
in the here and now.
In your Son's name we plead.
Hear our prayer.
Amen.

Chapter Notes

"Bring my sons ..." Isaiah 43:6-7.

"Bless the LORD ..." Psalm 104:1-2.

"He determines ..." Psalm 147:4-5.

"I blessed ..." Daniel 4:34-35.

"In the beginning ..." Hebrews 1:10-12.

"The LORD, the LORD God ..." Exodus 34:6- 8, *NASB*.

"To present ..." Colossians 1:22, *NET*.

"And we are put ..." William Blake, "The Little Black Boy," *Songs of Innocence and Songs of Experience* (New York: Dover, 1992), p. 10.

"Has a nation ..." Jeremiah 2:11-13.

"All this excellent ..." Jonathan Edwards, *Charity and Its Fruits*, sermon 8, in John Piper, *God's Passion for His Glory: Living the Vision of Jonathan Edwards With the Complete Text of "The End for Which God Created the World"* (Wheaton, IL: Crossway, 1998), p. 104.

"For all have sinned ..." Romans 3:23, *NASB*.

"I am the LORD ..." Isaiah 42:8, *NASB*.

"The heavens ..." Psalm 19:1, *NASB*.

"They feast ..." Psalm 36:8-9.

"This is my body ..." 1 Corinthians 11:24-25.

"Sin is the ..." John Piper, *God's Passion for His Glory: Living the Vision of Jonathan Edwards With the Complete Text of "The End for Which God Created the World"* (Wheaton, IL: Crossway, 1998), p. 81.

"I pray ..." Ephesians 1:17-19.

Chapter 2: Dirt

"God created ..." Genesis 1:28.

"O LORD, our Lord ..." Psalm 8:1,9, *NIV*.

"What are human ..." Psalm 8:4.

"God as Father ..." Robert W. Jenson, *Systematic Theology*, vol. 1 (New York: Oxford University Press, 1997), p. 226.

"For from Him ..." Romans 11:36, *NIV*.

"A theatre ..." John Calvin, *Commentary on Psalms* (Grand Rapids, MI: Wm. B. Eerdmans Publishing Co., 1950), 104:31.

"The creature's right ..." Karl Barth, *Church Dogmatics*, vol. 3, bk. 1, *The Doctrine of Creation*, trans. J. W. Edwards, O. Bussey, and H. Knight (New York: T & T Clark Publishers, 2004), p. 94.

"I am identical ..." Robert W. Jenson, *On Thinking the Human: Resolutions of Difficult Notions* (Grand Rapids, MI: Wm. B. Eerdmans Publishing Co., 2003), p. 71.

"At the very least ..." *Religion and Ethics NewsWeekly*, a PBS production of Thirteen/WNET, Profile of Barbara Brown Taylor, July 7, 2006. http://www.pbs.org/wnet/religionandethics/week945/profile.html. Used by permission.

"Your neighbor ..." C. S. Lewis, *The Weight of Glory and Other Addresses* (San Francisco: HarperSanFrancisco, 2000), p. 46.

"They forbid marriage ..." 1 Timothy 4:3-5.

"If spiritual transcendence ..." Lilian Calles Barger, *Eve's Revenge: Women and a Spirituality of the Body* (Grand Rapids, MI: Brazos Press, 2003), p. 65.

"Since the body ..." Barger, p. 101.

"In the creature's knowing ..." Jonathan Edwards, "The End for Which God Created the World," as included in Piper, *God's Passion for His Glory*, p. 247.

"Since the display ..." Piper, *God's Passion for His Glory*, p. 160.

Chapter 3: Way

"For God so loved ..." John 3:16, *KJV*.

"Without a doubt ..." 1 Timothy 3:16.

"Holy, Holy, Holy ..." Revelation 4:8.

"In the beginning ..." John 1:1,14, *TNIV*.

"There is no more ..." Dietrich Bonhoeffer, *Meditations on the Cross*, trans. Douglas W. Stott (Louisville, KY: Westminster John Knox Press, 1998), p. 57.

"But God ..." Ephesians 2:4-5.

"We believe ..." The Nicene Creed, as affirmed by the Council of Constantinople (A.D. 381), English Language Liturgical Commission translation.

"I am the resurrection ..." John 11:25.

"Jesus Christ is not ..." Bonhoeffer, *Meditations on the Cross*, p. 49.

"Look at my hands ..." Luke 24:39.

"There is one ..." 1 Timothy 2:5-6.

"Still wearing ..." Gerrit Scott Dawson, *Jesus Ascended: The Meaning of Christ's Continuing Incarnation* (Phillipsburg, NJ: P & R Publishing, 2004), p. 191.

"Worthy is the Lamb ..." Revelation 5:12-13, *TNIV*.

"Jesus underscored ..." Philip Yancey, *Rumors of Another World: What on Earth Are We Missing?* (Grand Rapids, MI: Zondervan Publishing House, 2003), p. 241.

"At Communion," by Madeleine L'Engle. Reprinted from *The Ordering of Love*. Copyright © 2005 by Crosswicks, Ltd. Used by permission of WaterBrook Press, Colorado Springs, CO. All rights reserved.

"The way of ascent ..." Tertullian, *Scorpiace*, in *Ante-Nicene Fathers*, vol. 3, ed. Alexander Roberts and James Donaldson (Peabody, MA: Hendrickson Publishers, 2004), p. 643.

"The kingdom of this world ..." Brian McLaren, *The Secret Message of Jesus: Uncovering the Truth that Could Change Everything* (Nashville, TN: W Publishing Group, 2006), p. 203.

"Demand eternities ..." Bonhoeffer, *Meditations on the Cross*, p. 55.

"The world says ..." Frederick Buechner, *The Faces of Jesus: A Life Story* (Orleans, MA: Paraclete Press, 2005), p. 61.

"We have been preoccupied ..." McLaren, *The Secret Message of Jesus*, p. 79.

"You are a letter ..." 2 Corinthians 3:3, *TNIV*.

"When the crucified ..." Jürgen Moltmann, *The Crucified God: The Cross of Christ as the Foundation and Criticism of Christian Theology*, trans. R. A. Wilson and John Bowden (Minneapolis, MN: Fortress Press, 1993), p. 205, emphasis added.

"While He was ..." Luke 24:51, *NASB*.

"The Advocate ..." John 14:26, *TNIV*.

"I go to prepare ..." John 14:2-3.

"His very absence ..." Frederick Buechner, *A Room Called Remember: Uncollected Pieces* (San Francisco: HarperSanFrancisco, 1992), p. 103.

"Lord of the Dance," by Jennifer Lynn Woodruff, "Lord of the Dance," reprinted from *Weavings: A Journal of the Christian Spiritual Life*, March/April 2002, Vol. XVII, No. 2 (Upper Room Ministries, 2002). Used by permission.

Chapter 4: Breathe

"Now the earth ..." Genesis 1:2, *NET*.
"When you take ..." Psalm 104:29-30, authors' translation.
"I will take ..." Numbers 11:17.
"I will pour out ..." Joel 2:28-29.
"And I will ask ..." John 14:16-17.
"Let anyone who is thirsty ..." John 7:37-38.
"And all of us ..." 2 Corinthians 3:18.
"The wind blows ..." John 3:8.
"To set the mind ..." Romans 8:6.
"It had always seemed ..." L. M. Montgomery, *Emily of New Moon* (New York: Laurel Leaf, 1983), p. 7.
"Do we still believe ..." Barbara Brown Taylor, *Home by Another Way* (Cambridge, MA: Cowley Publications, 1999), p. 145.
"When the goodness ..." Titus 3:5.
"This utterance ..." Robert W. Jenson, "Eighth Locus: The Holy Spirit," in *Christian Dogmatics*, vol. 2, ed. Carl E. Braaten and Robert W. Jenson (Minneapolis, MN: Fortress Press, 1984), p. 134.
"In Christ you also ..." Ephesians 1:13-14.
"So that the love ..." John 17:26.
"As co-heirs with Christ ..." Stanley Grenz, *The Named God and the Question of Being: A Trinitarian Theo-Ontology* (Louisville, KY: Westminster John Knox Pres, 2005), p. 338.
"Hope does not disappoint ..." Romans 5:5.
"Our perceptions ..." Maggie Ross, "Barking at Angels," *Weavings: A Journal of the Christian Spiritual Life*, vol. 21, no. 1 (January/February 2006), p. 16.
"There lives the dearest ..." Gerard Manley Hopkins, "God's Grandeur," *Poems* (Humphrey Milford, 1918; Bartleby.com, 1999). www.bartleby.com/122/.
"It is our business ..." Frederick Buechner, *The Longing for Home: Recollections and Reflections* (San Francisco: HarperSanFrancisco, 1996), p. 120.
"Ada judged ..." Annie Dillard, *The Living* (New York: HarperPerennial, 1992), pp. 374-75.

Chapter 5: Shift

"Hear, O Israel ..." Deuteronomy 6:4-9.
"We are far too ..." C. S. Lewis, *The Weight of Glory and Other Addresses* (San Francisco: HarperSanFrancisco, 2000), p. 26.
"Whom have I ..." Psalm 73:25-26.
"Forty days more ..." Jonah 3:4.
"The people of Ninevah ..." Jonah 3:5.
"Who knows ..." Jonah 3:9.
"This is why ..." Jonah 4:2-4.
"Which commandment ..." Mark 12:28-31.
"Seek their own ..." Martin Luther, "The Magnificat," in *Luther's Works*, vol. 21, ed. Jaroslav Pelikan (St. Louis, MO: Concordia Publishing House, 1986), p. 309.
"How marvelous ..." Charles H. Gabriel, "I Stand Amazed in the Presence," in *Praises*, by Edwin O. Excell (Chicago: E. O. Excell, 1905).
"To be sure ..." Augustine, *The City of God Against the Pagans*, bk. 14, chap. 13, Cambridge Texts in the History of Political Thought, ed. R. W. Dyson (New York: Cambridge University Press, 1998), p. 609.
"God remains gloriously all-satisfying ..." John Piper, *Desiring God* (Sisters, OR: Multnomah Publishers, 2003), p. 12.

"You called ..." Augustine, *The Confessions*, trans. Henry Chadwick (New York: Oxford University Press, 1991), p. 201.

"Those who find ..." Matthew 10:39.

"Worship is idolatry ..." Marva J. Dawn, *A Royal "Waste" of Time: The Splendor of Worshiping God and Being Church for the World* (Grand Rapids, MI: Wm. B. Eerdmans Publishing Co., 1999), p. 11.

"So if you have been raised ..." Colossians 3:1,9-10,14.

"I'm going to spend ..." Clint Black, "Spend My Time" (Equity Music Group, 2004).

"Let's just suppose ..." Buechner, *A Room Called Remember*, p. 89.

"Lay ourselves ..." Jonathan Edwards, "Sacrament Sermon on Canticles 5:1," 1729, sermon manuscript, Beinecke Library, Yale University.

"A shrub in the desert ..." Eugene Peterson, *Subversive Spirituality* (Grand Rapids, MI: Wm. B. Eerdmans Publishing Co., 1997), p. 82.

"Restore to us ..." Psalm 51:12 (paraphrase).

"Abbot Lot ..." Thomas Merton, ed., *The Wisdom of the Desert*, quoted in Kathleen Norris, *Dakota: A Spiritual Geography* (Boston: Mariner Books, 2001), p. 123.

Chapter 6: Joy

"Is there a single ..." Leif Enger, *Peace Like a River* (New York: Grove Press, 2001), p. 311.

"Divinity is not playful ..." Annie Dillard, *Pilgrim at Tinker Creek* (New York: Harper Perennial Modern Classics, 1998), p. 275.

"I will exalt you ..." Psalm 145, *TNIV* (throughout the chapter).

"Morning Person," by Vassar Miller (New Orleans Poetry Journal Press, 1984). Reprinted by permission.

"Joyful, joyful ..." Henry van Dyke, "Joyful, Joyful, We Adore Thee."

"The sacred does not ..." Daniel Taylor, *In Search of Sacred Places: Looking for Wisdom on Celtic Holy Islands* (St. Paul, MN: Bog Walk Press, 2005), p. 60.

"The Peace of Wild Things," by Wendell Berry. From *The Selected Poems of Wendell Berry* (Counterpoint, 1999). Reprinted by permission of Counterpoint Press, a member of Perseus Books Group.

"Re-text us," by Walter Brueggemann. From *Awed to Heaven, Rooted in Earth: Prayers of Walter Brueggemann* (Augsburg Fortress, 2003). Reprinted by permission.

"For the Lord is ..." Psalm 95:3-7, *NASB*.

"Tell all the Truth ..." Emily Dickinson, No. 1129.

"Old Folks Laugh," copyright © 1990 by Maya Angelou, from I SHALL NOT BE MOVED by Maya Angelou. Used by permission of Random House, Inc.

"I can't stand ..." Taylor, *In Search of Sacred Places*, p. 116.

"Sometimes in their chanting ..." Thomas Moore, *Meditations: On the Monk Who Dwells in Daily Life* (New York: HarperCollins Publishers, 1994), p. 44.

"To delight ..." Piper, *God's Passion for His Glory*, p. 108.

Chapter 7: Rope

"The love of God ..." Frederick M. Lehman, "The Love of God" (1917).

"I pray that ..." Ephesians 3:16-19.

"Because they are nigh ..." Thomas Aquinas, *Summa Theologica*, second part of the second part, question 44, article 7 (New York: Benziger Brothers, 1947).

"I was being asked ..." Donald Miller, *Blue like Jazz* (Nashville, TN: Thomas Nelson, 2003), p. 183.

"This is my commandment ..." John 15:12-14.

"All of our lives ..." F. LeRon Shults and Steven J. Sandage, *The Faces of Forgiveness: Searching for Wholeness and Salvation* (Grand Rapids, MI: Baker Academic, 2003), p. 216.

"Owe no one ..." Romans 13:8-10.

"The command of God ..." Karl Barth, *Church Dogmatics*, vol. 3, bk. 4, *The Doctrine of Creation*, trans. A. T. Mackay, T. H. L. Parker, H. Knight, H. A. Kennedy, and J. Marks (New York: T & T Clark Publishers, 2004), p. 293.

"In this is love ..." 1 John 4:10-12.

"You have heard ..." Matthew 5:43-44 (paraphrase).

"What is both ..." Frederick Buechner, *Wishful Thinking: A Theological ABC* (San Francisco: HarperSanFrancisco, 1973), p. 33.

"To love somebody ..." Leonard Pitts, Jr., "A Phone Rings, and Our Lives Are on Hold," *Miami Herald* (February 24, 2006), p. 1B.

"To turn Christianity ..." Theodore Runyon, "Holiness as the Renewal of the Image of God in the Individual and Society," in *Embodied Holiness: Toward a Corporate Theology of Spiritual Growth*, ed. Samuel Powell and Michael Lodahl (Downers Grove, IL: InterVarsityPress, 1999), p. 83.

"I appeal to you ..." Romans 12:1-2.

"Be kind to one another ..." Ephesians 4:32; 5:2.

"I am as Thou art ..." Karl Barth, *Church Dogmatics*, vol. 3, bk. 2, *The Doctrine of Creation*, trans. H. Knight, G. W. Bromiley, J. K. S. Reid, R. H. Fuller (New York: T & T Clark Publishers, 2004), p. 249.

"Your life ..." Frederick Buechner, *The Magnificent Defeat* (San Francisco: HarperSanFrancisco, 1966), p. 143.

"It is the task ..." Jürgen Moltmann, *How I Have Changed: Reflections on Thirty Years of Theology*, (Harrisburg, PA: Trinity Press International, 1997), p. 110.

"Neither death ..." Romans 8:38-39.

"Teach us to care ..." Eugene Peterson, *Subversive Spirituality* (Grand Rapids, MI: Wm. B. Eerdmans Publishing Co., 1997), p. 167.

Chapter 8: Space

"Grace teaches ..." Philip Yancey, *What's So Amazing About Grace?* (Grand Rapids, MI: Zondervan, 1997), p. 280.

"Gracious is the Lord ..." Psalm 116:5-9.

"He destined us ..." Ephesians 1:5-7.

"My God, thought Hayes ..." Michael Malone, *Handling Sin* (Naperville, IL: Sourcebooks Inc., 2001), p. 521.

"You who live ..." Psalm 91:1-2.

"After the Saturday Liturgy at Montfort," by Madeleine L'Engle. Reprinted from *The Ordering of Love*. Copyright © 2005 by Crosswicks, Ltd. Used by permission of WaterBrook Press, Colorado Springs, CO. All rights reserved.

"Salvation is a word ..." Barbara Brown Taylor, *Leaving Church: A Memoir of Faith* (San Francisco: HarperSanFrancisco, 2006), p. 226.

"The final break-through ..." Dietrich Bonhoeffer, *Life Together*, trans. John W. Doberstein (San Francisco: HarperSanFrancisco, 1954), p. 110.

"Rarely will anyone ..." Romans 5:7-8.

"The opposite of sin ..." Yancey, *What's So Amazing About Grace?* p. 206.

"These last men ..." Matthew 20:12, *NASB*.

"Is it not lawful ..." Matthew 20:15, *NASB*.

"Grace is not about finishing ..." Yancey, *What's So Amazing About Grace?* pp. 61-62.

"And bringing up ..." Flannery O'Connor, "Revelation," in *The Complete Stories of Flannery O'Connor* (New York: Farrar, Straus, and Giroux, 1971), p. 508.

"If then there is ..." Philippians 2:1-5.

"Salvation happens every time ..." Barbara Brown Taylor, *Leaving Church*, p. 115.

"Little by little compassionate love ..." Buechner, *The Longing for Home*, pp. 120-21.

"Let no evil talk ..." Ephesians 4:29-5:2.

Chapter 9: Gift

"The word forgiveness ..." Herbert Lockyer, *Everything Jesus Taught*, vol. 1 (New York: Harper and Row Publishers, 1976), p. 78.

"Every perfect gift ..." Steve Green, "That's Where the Joy Comes From" (Navarre Corporation, 1985).

"I will cleanse ..." Jeremiah 33:8-9.

"By his great mercy ..." 1 Peter 1:3-4.

"Take words ..." Hosea 14:2-3.

"The Pharisee ..." Luke 18:11-14.

"Grace means ..." Yancey, *What's So Amazing About Grace?* p. 71.

"But flesh ..." Psalm 78:39.

"Forgiveness is the name of love ..." Henri Nouwen, "Forgiveness: The Name of Love in a Wounded World," *Weavings: A Journal of the Christian Spiritual Life*, vol. 7, no. 2 (March/April 1992), p. 15.

"The will to give ..." Miroslav Volf, *Exclusion and Embrace: A Theological Exploration of Identity, Otherness, and Reconciliation* (Nashville, TN: Abingdon Press, 1996), p. 29.

"So how do I love ..." Marilyn Chandler McEntyre, "How Do I Love Thee? A Letter to My Enemies," *Weavings: A Journal of the Christian Spiritual Life*, vol. 21, no. 2 (March/April 2006), p. 10.

"I forgave you ..." Matthew 18:32-33.

"When we forgive ..." Lewis B. Smedes, *Forgive and Forget: Healing the Hurts We Don't Deserve* (San Francisco: Harper & Row, 1984), p. 152.

"Costly acts ..." Volf, *Exclusion and Embrace*, p. 306.

"Any movement ..." Lewis B. Smedes, *How Can It Be All Right When Everything Is All Wrong?* (San Francisco: Harper & Row, 1982), pp. 351-52.

"I will heal ..." Hosea 14:4-7.

Chapter 10: Fool

"Where there is love ..." Mother Teresa, statement sent to the Cairo International Conference on Population and Development on September 9, 1994. http://www.ewtn.com/library/ISSUES/MTCAIRO.HTM (accessed March 2007).

"We do not live ..." Romans 14:7-8.

"To worship God ..." Buechner, *Wishful Thinking*, p 110.

"For even the Son ..." Mark 10:45, *TNIV*.

"I have said ..." John 15:11-13.

"For while we live ..." 2 Corinthians 4:11-12,15.

"This experience tells us ..." Henri Nouwen, *The Wounded Healer: Ministry in Contemporary Society* (Garden City, NY: Image Books/Doubleday, 1990), pp. 91-92.

"It is a great loss ..." Father Daniel Homan, O.S.B., and Lonni Collins Pratt, *Radical Hospitality: Benedict's Way of Love* (Brester, MA: Paraclete Press, 2002), p. xxxvii.

"We all have weapons ..." Homan and Pratt, pp. 127-28.

"To sacrifice ..." Buechner, *Wishful Thinking*, p. 114.

"Let mutual love ..." Hebrews 13:1-3.

"What I Learned from My Mother," from *Sleeping Preacher*, by Julia Kasdorf © 1992. Reprinted by permission of the University of Pittsburgh Press.

"Now concerning our brother ..." 1 Corinthians 16:12.

"By my rules ..." Barbara Brown Taylor, *Leaving Church*, p. 119.

"But who am I ..." 1 Chronicles 29:14-16.

"He who is mightier ..." Luke 3:16, *NASB*.

"Such is the confidence ..." 2 Corinthians 3:4-6.

"I appeal to you ..." Romans 12:1,9,13,18.

"Zaccheus, hurry ..." Luke 19:5, *NASB*.

"Therefore my heart ..." Psalm 16:9-11.

"Ascribe to the Lord ..." Psalm 96:8.

"What's lost is nothing ..." Frederick Buechner, *Godric* (San Francisco: HarperSanFrancisco, 1980), p. 96.

Chapter 11: Sight

"Our Father ..." Matthew 6:9-10, *KJV*.

"The Lord looks ..." Psalm 33:13-21.

"Truly, truly ..." John 5:24, *NASB*.

"An inheritance ..." 1 Peter 1:4, *NASB*.

"The resurrection hope ..." Jürgen Moltmann, *The Coming of God: Christian Eschatology*, trans. Margaret Kohl (Minneapolis, MN: Fortress Press, 1996), p. 66.

"Expectation yoked ..." Everett F. Harrison, "Hope," in *The International Standard Bible Encyclopedia*, vol. 2, ed. Geoffrey W. Bromiley (Grand Rapids, MI: Wm. B. Eerdmans Publishing Co., 1982), p. 752.

"Groan inwardly ..." Romans 8:23-25.

"For now we see ..." 1 Corinthians 13:12.

"Although you have ..." 1 Peter 1:8-9,21.

"We have this hope ..." Hebrews 6:19-20.

"Through all the bright ..." "A Plagued Journey," copyright © 1983 by Maya Angelou, from SHAKER, WHY DON'T YOU SING? by Maya Angelou. Used by permission of Random House, Inc.

"Where would I be ..." Psalm 27:13, *NET*.

"The notion ..." Moltmann, *The Coming of God*, pp. 50, 53.

"Let us draw near ..." Hebrews 10:19-25, *NASB*.

"The horizon leans ..." "On the Pulse of Morning," copyright © 1993 by Maya Angelou, from ON THE PULSE OF MORNING by Maya Angelou. Used by permission of Random House, Inc.

"And the true vision ..." Gregory of Nyssa, *The Life of Moses*, in *The Essential Writings of Christian Mysticism*, ed. Bernard McGinn (New York: Modern Library, 2006), p. 18.

"See, the home of God ..." Revelation 21:3-4.

"Then the angel ..." Revelation 22:1,5.

"May the God of hope ..." Romans 15:13.

"God Speaks in Blue," by Luci Shaw. Copyright © 2006 by Luci Shaw. Published in *What the Light Was Like*, by Luci Shaw (La Porte, IN: WordFarm, 2006). Used with permission from WordFarm, www.wordfarm.net.

Chapter 12: The Practice of Life with God

"For God so loved the world ..." John 3:16, *KJV*.

"Life is a tornado watch ..." Q9 Advertising, advertisement for Fireman's Fund Insurance, n.d.

About the Authors

LifeSpace is an ongoing creative project that encompasses this book, *salons* where interesting people gather to explore a particular topic, weekly learning series in churches around the country and an interactive website. The future vision for the project even includes a retreat center under a big sky.

As co-founders, Joni Powers and Bob Pyne desire to create a wide space for people to practice this life with God. They view themselves as the loose facilitators of an organic community of conversation. That conversation rests on particular beliefs on who God is, why we are created and how we love God and others well. The LifeSpace project is meant to be fluid with room to respond as the Holy Spirit leads.

• • • • • from Joni

The strangest thing happened when I went to seminary. The big sky God I brought with me became smaller and smaller. I put a box around God and studied Him like a lab specimen. I could barely breathe. LifeSpace developed as a desperate response to that suffocation. Its message pushes against the boundaries, expanding into the boundless glory of God.

Teaching is my passion. I teach literally hands on. Chaining me to a podium feels like prison. I roam about, touch shoulders, laugh hysterically, cry often and generally fling the love of God on my audience. The disembodied aspect of writing a book has been a great challenge. I want all the readers to come lollygag with us for a while!

• • • • • from Bob

The whisper of LifeSpace can be heard in every conversation I engage in or class I teach. The message is life's one really big idea for me. LifeSpace sums up the major lessons of my own experience. Its concepts reflect my passionate belief in an expansive, fully human life centered in the glorious, infinite God.

I am now embarking on a new phase of my career. The opportunity to work with African Leadership and Reconciliation Ministries brings together my love of teaching and my desire to live with a broad horizon before me. The LifeSpace concepts resonate no matter where they are heard. God graciously allows us to participate in what is really real about the practice of life with God.

● ● ● ● ●

Joni and Bob represent a unique partnership in their LifeSpace collaboration. They are the yin and the yang of style in writing and teaching. They share a love of storytelling and of good books. The hardest part of writing together is deciding which fabulous words of other writers not to quote!

Bob thinks an afternoon cruising through a book by someone such as Karl Barth or Frederick Buechner borders on perfection. Throw in a run down a wooded path and all is well. Joni will opt for some adventurous adrenaline rush followed by a robust red wine and laughter over dinner.

Both are raising their families in Dallas, Texas. They infect their teenagers with the international travel bug whenever possible. Their spouses, Tim and Julie, are known as their greatest assets. Both families are longtime members of a local nondenominational church, where the LifeSpace concepts were first aired out in a weekly teaching series.

 LifeSpace

Join the LifeSpace dialogue at
www.lifespaceonline.com.

*Joni and Bob teach the LifeSpace
concepts at retreats and conferences
as well as in weekly series in local churches.
Visit the website to find out more
and book an engagement.*

A Spiritual Journey for Those Who May Have Given Up on Church But Not on God

A Place for Skeptics
Scott Larson and *Chris Mitchell*
ISBN 08307.37057

If you, or someone you know, are reconsidering some of the larger questions of life, then this is the book for you. This unique guidebook is a 30-day spiritual journey that examines questions about God, the Bible, faith and Jesus. *A Place for Skeptics* is written as a conversation, engaging Christian truth in a relevant, nonconfrontational style. Modern questions and doubts intersect with ancient confessions of the Christian faith in this provocative book of reflections. What results is the opportunity to consider the validity of Christianity and what it may mean to nurture and grow a real faith.

For "interested skeptics" who are not yet ready to come to church but are considering it, as well as new believers looking for something to put them on the path of regular reflection and prayer.

Engaging the Silence of Unanswered Prayer

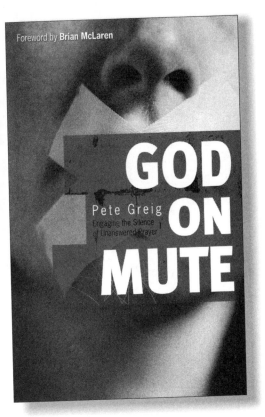

Foreword by **Brian McLaren**

GOD ON MUTE

Pete Greig
Engaging the Silence of Unanswered Prayer

God on Mute
978.08307.43247

Pete Greig, the acclaimed author of *Red Moon Rising*, has written his most intensely personal and honest book yet in *God on Mute*, a work born out of his wife Samie's fight for her life. Greig asks the timeless questions of what it means to suffer and to pray and to suffer through the silence because your prayers seem unanswered. This silence, Greig relates, is the hardest thing. The world collapses. Then all goes quiet. Words can't explain, don't fit, won't work. People avoid you and don't know what to say. So you turn to Him and you pray. You need Him more than ever before. But some-how...even God Himself seems on mute. In this heart-searching, honest and deeply profound book, Pete Greig looks at the hard side of prayer, how to respond when there seem to be no answers and how to cope with those who seek to interpret our experience for us. Here is a story of faith, hope and love beyond all understanding.

[24-7 TITLES]
WWW.24-7PRAYER.COM